the chinese cuisine I love

the chinese cuisine I love

by JULES J. BOND

LEON AMIEL • PUBLISHER
NEW YORK

Published by
LEON AMIEL • PUBLISHER
NEW YORK
ISBN 0-8148-0678-3
©Copyright 1977, by Leon Amiel • Publisher
Printed in the United States of America

Foreword

Chinese cuisine is the oldest in the world and one of the most refined. When most of the world's population was still cooking game and fish over open fires, the Chinese had already developed complicated and imaginative ways to prepare food for the delight of the palate and the eye.

With all the variety and refinement of Chinese cooking, it is also the most economical. Vast population, frequent floods and other natural catastrophes throughout China's recorded history have forced the careful husbanding of foods and the use of herbs, spices and condiments to enhance and vary the available basic foodstuffs.

In recent years the interest in Chinese food has grown tremendously in America. The regional foods of China — Hunan, Szechuan, Mongolia, Canton and many others — have their devotees.

We have tried to present in this book a great variety of recipes, most of them quite easy to prepare. The ingredients are available in most markets, either fresh, canned or frozen.

We have given exact measurements and cooking times. However, cooking is an enjoyable art, and it is one of the great joys of cooking to experiment with and to vary recipes to suit your own taste. Take the ones in this book as the base for your enjoyment of Chinese food.

Bon appetit!

Jules Bond

Table of Contents

The Publishers give grateful acknowledgements to: The National Rice Council, which provided the photograph shown on the front cover; Josh Konecky, who took all other photographs; and Roy Jensen, who coordinated the production of this book.

LIST OF COLOR PLATES

Notes

INGREDIENTS

Bamboo shoots and **water chestnuts** are available in cans almost everywhere.

Broth, beef or chicken. Some very good canned brands are readily available in all markets and can be used in all recipes. Condensed broth is not recommended.

Sherry: use a medium dry sherry of the Amontillado type. Domestic sherry of this type is usually labeled "Cocktail sherry."

Soy sauce: use Chinese soy sauce only. Other types of soy sauce are quite different and not recommended.

Hoisin and Oyster sauces are available in all Chinese food stores. Or make your own oyster sauce (p. 153).

Rice: use Carolina, Patna (Texas) or any other long-grain raw rice. Precooked rice is not suitable for Chinese cooking.

EQUIPMENT AND PROCEDURES

The Wok is the most versatile of all cooking vessels. Ideal not only for stir-frying, it can be used covered for braising, stewing and steaming. Used on an electric range the wok is somewhat less desirable and a regular skillet is preferable. The amount of oil used for frying given in the recipes will probably have to be increased slightly if a skillet is used instead of a wok.

Steaming: There are three ways of steaming food. Either in a special Chinese-type steamer, or by setting a bowl or dish containing food on a rack over boiling water, or by placing the bowl directly in boiling water.

Bamboo Shoot Salad
(for 4)

2 cups bamboo shoots
4 stalks celery, white part
3 tbsp. oil
1 tbsp. soy sauce

1 tsp. sugar
1 tsp. sherry
$\frac{1}{3}$ cup chicken broth
salt and white pepper
1 tbsp. minced scallions

Cut bamboo shoots in 1½ inch strips. Slice celery lengthwise in 1 inch wide strips and cut to 3 inch lengths. Add oil to a saucepan, stir-fry bamboo shoots and celery for 2 minutes. Combine soy sauce, sugar, sherry, chicken broth, salt and pepper, add to saucepan, cover and simmer for about 15 minutes, until vegetables are cooked but still firm. Refrigerate until chilled, sprinkle with scallions.

Bean Sprout Salad
(for 4)

1 lb. bean sprouts
¼ cup scallions, green part, chopped
2 tbsp. soy sauce

1 tsp. sugar
1 tbsp. vinegar
½ tsp. sesame oil
salt and pepper to taste

Wash bean sprouts, drain and place in a bowl. Pour boiling water over them and let stand 3 minutes. Drain well, put in a serving bowl, add scallions, blend all other ingredients, add to bowl, toss gently and chill.

Bean Sprout and Ham Salad
(for 6)

1 lb. bean sprouts
½ lb. cooked ham, cut into
   thin strips
2 tbsp. soy sauce
1 tbsp. vinegar

1 tbsp. oil
small pinch of powdered ginger
1 tsp. sugar
salt and pepper to taste

Wash bean sprouts. Pour boiling water over them and let stand for one minute. Drain well. Mix with ham strips. Blend all other ingredients, pour over bean sprouts and ham, mix and chill for 1 hour.

Celery Salad
(for 4)

6 tender celery stalks
1 cup chicken broth
½ cup watercress
1 tbsp. soy sauce
1 tbsp. vinegar

1 tbsp. fresh ginger root,
   minced (opt.)
½ tsp. sugar
salt to taste
½ tsp. sesame oil

Trim and string celery stalks, cut in half lengthwise and then in 1½ inch pieces. Trim tough stems off watercress and cut cress in 1 inch pieces. Bring chicken broth to boil, add celery and cook covered for 2 minutes, until slightly softened. Drain, cool, put in a bowl. Add watercress. Combine all other ingredients, add to vegetables, toss and chill.

Spinach Salad
(for 4)

1 lb. spinach
1 tbsp. vinegar
1½ tbsp. soy sauce
1 tsp. sherry

1 tbsp. oil
1 scallion, minced
2 water chestnuts, sliced thin
Salt and pepper to taste

Wash spinach well, discard coarse stems. Cut leaves into thin strips. Put in a bowl, pour boiling water over spinach, let stand for half a minute. Drain well, rinse quickly with cold water and drain again. Combine all other ingredients, blend gently with spinach and chill well.

Chinese Cucumber Salad
(for 6)

2 large cucumbers
2 scallions, minced
1½ tbsp. soy sauce
2 tsp. sherry

2 tsp. vinegar
1½ tsp. oil
1 tsp. sugar
1 small clove garlic, crushed

Peel cucumbers, slice lengthwise in half and scoop out seeds. Slice thin and put in a bowl. Blend all other ingredients, mix with cucumbers and refrigerate for an hour before serving.

Stuffed Clams

(for 6)

24 clams
¼ lb. cooked ham, minced
1 tsp. minced fresh ginger
½ clove garlic, minced
3 tbsp. minced onion
1 tbsp. soy sauce

1 tbsp. sherry
½ tsp. sugar
½ tsp. salt
¼ cup strained clam juice
3 tbsp. oil

Scrub clams, place in a pan and steam open. Remove the clams from shells and reserve half the empty shells. Chop clams and blend with ham, garlic, onions, ginger, soy sauce, sherry, salt and sugar. Fill 24 half clam shells with the mixture and place in a baking dish. Mix clam juice and oil, sprinkle over clams and bake in 400° oven for 20 minutes.

Steamed Stuffed Clams
(for 6)

2 dozen small clams
½ lb. lean pork
2 scallions
½ clove garlic
1 tbsp. soy sauce

1 tbsp. sherry
1 tsp. chinese parsley (opt.)
½ tsp. sugar
pinch of salt

Steam clams open, remove the meat and reserve the shells. Mince clams, together with pork, scallions, garlic and parsley and combine with all other ingredients. Stuff the half shells, place them on a shallow dish and steam for 15 to 20 minutes.

Shrimp and Water Chestnut Patties

(for 6)

1 lb. shrimp, shelled, deveined
and minced
1 cup water chestnuts, cut
in small dice
2 tbsp. soy sauce
1 tbsp. sherry
1 tsp. sugar

¼ tsp. hot red pepper
1 large clove garlic, crushed
1 tsp. ginger, shredded
3 eggs, lightly beaten
3 tbsp. cornstarch
oil for deep frying

Combine all ingredients, blend well. Cover the bottom of a heavy skillet with about 2 inches of oil, heat and drop the mixture, spoonful by spoonful in the oil. Fry — a few at a time — until golden brown.

Shrimp Toast
(for 4)

½ lb. medium shrimps shelled and deveined
1 thin slice fresh ginger root
2 eggs
1 tbsp. onion, minced
1 clove garlic, minced
1 tsp. cornstarch
1 tsp. sherry
pinch of sugar
salt and pepper to taste
4 slices firm, stale bread
oil for deep frying
2 tbsp. minced smoked ham

Chop shrimps and ginger root very fine. Beat the eggs until frothy. Blend shrimp, ginger, onion, garlic, cornstarch, sherry, sugar, salt and pepper and a little more than half of the beaten eggs. Trim the crust off the bread and spread the slices with the shrimp mixture. Cut the slices into triangles and brush with the remaining egg. Heat the oil for deep frying. Put the bread triangles, shrimp side down, a few at a time into the hot oil and fry for about a minute. Turn them carefully and fry 45 seconds longer. Drain on paper towels and sprinkle with ham before serving.

Stuffed Mushrooms
(for 4)

¼ lb. shrimp, shelled,
   deveined, and minced
¼ lb. lean pork, ground
1 scallion, white part, minced
4 water chestnuts, minced
1 egg white, lightly beaten
1 tbsp. cornstarch

salt and pepper to taste
1 tsp. minced fresh ginger root
1 tbsp. soy sauce
1 tbsp. sherry
16 large dried Chinese
   mushroom caps

Wash mushrooms under running water, soak in warm water for 6 hours. Remove and discard stems, gently squeeze water out of caps.

Combine shrimp, pork and water chestnuts, mix gently. Blend in the egg white, add cornstarch and all other ingredients except mushrooms. Blend and fill the mushroom caps with the mixture.

Place in a steamer and steam for 45 minutes.

Stir-fried Pork and Vegetables—See page 97 for recipe.→

Stir-fried Chicken and Vegetables—See page 59 for recipe.→

Chicken on Skewers
(for 6)

1 chicken breast, skinned
  and boned
½ lb. lean bacon, cut in
  1-inch squares
4 water chestnuts, sliced
  very thin
3 tbsp. soy sauce

1 tbsp. sherry
1 tbsp. brown sugar
¼ tsp. hot mustard
1 tsp. shredded ginger
1 scallion, minced
1 clove garlic, crushed

Glaze: 2 tbsp. honey
      1½ tbsp. soy sauce
      ½ tbsp. sherry

    Combine all ingredients except chicken, water chestnuts, bacon and glaze. Marinate the chicken breast in this mixture for 3 hours. Then remove from marinade, pat dry and slice very thin, across the grain. Thread alternating pieces of chicken, bacon and water chestnut on small skewers, brush with glaze and broil or deep fry.

←*Chicken and Cashew Nuts*—See page 57 for recipe.

Drunken Chicken
(for 4)

2 whole chicken breasts,
  boned
water
2 scallions, chopped

1 clove garlic, crushed
2 slices fresh ginger root
2 tsp. salt
sherry

    Put water, scallions, garlic, and ginger root in a saucepan and bring to a boil. Add chicken breasts, cover and simmer for 10 minutes. Remove from heat and let stand covered for 15 minutes. Drain chicken, remove and discard skin, sprinkle chicken with salt and put in a jar with tight fitting cover. Fill jar with sherry, enough to cover the chicken, and refrigerate for 3 to 4 days. Before serving, drain and cut into bite size cubes. Serve cold.

Chicken and Mushroom Soup
(for 4)

1 chicken breast, boned
  and skinned
5 medium, firm fresh
  mushrooms
½ cup bamboo shoots
2 tbsp. sherry

6 cups chicken broth
1 scallion, chopped
1½ tsp. cornstarch
1 tsp. salt
⅛ tsp. sesame oil (opt.)

  Slice chicken into thin, 2 inch long slices. Slice mushrooms and bamboo shoots. Dilute cornstarch in 2 tablespoons of broth. Bring broth to boil, add chicken and vegetables, simmer covered for about 5 minutes; add sherry, salt, cornstarch, blend well; add scallion and bring to a simmer, stir until soup thickens. Sprinkle with sesame oil before serving.

Chicken Sub Gum Soup
(for 6)

1½ tbsp. oil
1 chicken breast, boned, skinned and shredded
½ cup celery, white part, sliced
½ cup fresh mushrooms, sliced

7 cups chicken broth
4 water chestnuts, diced
½ cup bean sprouts, washed and drained
1 egg, lightly beaten
salt and pepper to taste

Heat oil in a heavy saucepan, stir-fry chicken for one minute, add celery and mushrooms, stir-fry one minute, add water chestnuts and stir-fry 30 seconds longer. Add broth, sprouts, salt and pepper, bring to a boil, cover and cook gently for 10 minutes. Add beaten egg, stir quickly and serve.

Cucumber Soup
(for 4)

2 medium cucumbers
¼ lb. lean pork
1 clove garlic, minced

4 cups chicken broth
½ tsp. vinegar
2 eggs

Peel cucumbers and cut in half lengthwise. Remove seeds and slice crosswise ¼ inch thick. Cut pork diagonally into ¼ inch thick slices. Beat eggs until creamy. Heat stock, when boiling add cucumbers, garlic, meat and vinegar. Cover and simmer for 10 minutes. Remove from heat and add, drop by drop, the beaten eggs.

Egg Drop Soup I
(for 4)

1 egg
½ tsp. sherry
3 cups chicken broth
pinch of sugar

¼ tsp. sesame oil
salt to taste
¼ tsp. finely minced garlic
1 scallion, white part, minced
2 tsp. chives, chopped

Beat egg with sherry until frothy. Put broth in a saucepan, bring to a simmer and stir in sugar, salt, garlic and sesame oil. Slip egg mixture into broth and stir vigorously until thin threads are formed. Add scallions, stir and serve in individual bowls, garnished with chives.

Egg Drop Soup II
(for 4)

½ chicken breast, boned and skinned
¼ lb. lean pork
1 tbsp. cornstarch
2 tbsp. sherry
1 egg white
⅓ cup fresh mushrooms sliced
2 stalks celery, white part, minced

2 scallions, minced
2 spinach leaves, shredded
⅓ cup bamboo shoots, shredded
6 cups chicken broth
1 tbsp. cornstarch
3 tbsp. broth
1 tbsp. vinegar
salt and white pepper to taste
2 eggs, beaten

Blend 1 tablespoon cornstarch, sherry and egg white. Shred chicken and pork and coat with cornstarch mixture. Heat stock, add mushrooms, spinach leaves, celery and bamboo shoots, bring to a boil, cover and simmer 3 minutes. Add one tablespoon cornstarch diluted with broth and vinegar, salt and pepper, stir until soup starts to thicken. Add pork and chicken and cook stirring for 2 minutes. Pour in beaten eggs, a little at a time, stirring vigorously until egg threads have set. Sprinkle with scallions and serve.

Hot and Sour Soup
(for 4)

4 dried Chinese mushrooms
¼ lb. lean pork
¼ cup bamboo shoots
2 bean curd cakes
1 egg
1½ tbsp. cornstarch
4 cups chicken broth

2 tbsp. water
1 tbsp. sherry
2 tbsp. white vinegar
1½ tbsp. soy sauce
pinch of cayenne pepper
salt to taste
1 scallion, minced

Soak mushrooms for 30 minutes in warm water, squeeze dry, discard stems. Cut into thin strips. Cut pork across grain into ¼ inch thick slices, then into very narrow strips. Cut bamboo shoots and bean curds into thin strips. Beat egg lightly. Put broth in a saucepan and bring to boil. Add pork and mushrooms and simmer for 10 minutes. Add bamboo shoots and curd, simmer 5 more minutes. Add sherry, vinegar, soy sauce, salt and cayenne pepper, and the cornstarch dissolved in water. Simmer and stir until the soup has thickened. Then add very slowly the beaten egg, stir for a few seconds, add scallions and serve.

Fish Soup
(for 4)

¾ lb. filet of flounder
1 tbsp. cornstarch
2 tbsp. soy sauce
1 tbsp. sherry
⅓ cup fresh mushrooms, sliced

5 cups chicken broth
⅓ cup celery, white part, finely diced
½ tsp. minced ginger root (opt.)
salt and white pepper

Cut fish in one inch squares. Dilute cornstarch with 1 tablespoon each of soy sauce and sherry, add to fish and blend. Put chicken broth in a saucepan, bring to a boil, add celery and mushrooms, the remaining tablespoon of soy sauce, ginger, salt and pepper and simmer covered for 5 minutes. Add fish, stir and simmer uncovered for 5 minutes.

Fishball Soup
(for 6)

½ lb. flounder or whiting filet, minced

¼ lb. lean pork, finely ground

2 tbsp. soy sauce

1 tbsp. sherry

2 scallions, white part only, chopped

½ tsp. ginger root, minced

salt and pepper to taste

1 small clove garlic, crushed

1 egg, lightly beaten

2 tbsp. cornstarch

4 cups chicken broth

2 cups water

Mix all ingredients except broth and water. Blend well and form into small balls. Bring broth and water to a boil, drop the balls gently into the simmering liquid and cook covered for 15 minutes.

Shrimp Soup

(for 4)

1½ cups shelled raw shrimp
2 scallions, cut in ½ inch
   pieces
1 slice fresh ginger root,
   minced
1 tbsp. oil
2 tbsp. sherry

5 cups chicken broth
salt and white pepper
   to taste
1 large egg, beaten
1 tbsp. cornstarch
2 tbsp. broth

Cut shrimp in smallish chunks. Heat oil in a saucepan, add ginger and scallions, stir-fry ½ minute, add shrimp and stir-fry 1 minute. Add chicken broth and sherry, bring to a boil, season with salt and pepper, reduce heat, add beaten egg and stir or whisk for a few seconds; add cornstarch diluted in stock, stir until soup thickens and is smooth. Do not let boil.

Peking Soup
(for 6)

2 tbsp. oil
¼ lb. lean pork
1 cup fresh mushrooms, sliced
½ cup diced carrots
1 cup diced celery
6 cups chicken broth
1 egg, lightly beaten

½ cup spinach, washed, trimmed
   and coarsely chopped
2 tbsp. cornstarch
1 tbsp. soy sauce
2 tbsp. broth
salt and pepper to taste

Put oil in a heavy saucepan, cut pork into thin strips and stir-fry for 2 minutes. Add carrots, stir-fry a minute, add mushrooms and celery and fry until vegetables are almost cooked. Add chicken broth, cover and simmer for 10 minutes. Then add spinach, simmer for another 2 minutes, add egg and stir quickly until threads form, blend cornstarch, soy sauce and broth, stir into soup to thicken. Season with salt and pepper.

Pungent Soup
(for 6)

1 small chicken breast, boned, skinned and cut in strips

$^1/_3$ lb. lean pork, cut in thin strips

4 cups chicken broth

2 cups water

2 scallions, cut in 1-inch pieces

1 tsp. ginger, shredded

2 tbsp. sherry

$^1/_3$ cup vinegar

1 clove garlic, minced

½ tsp. hot red pepper

salt to taste

4 tbsp. water

3 tbsp. cornstarch

Combine broth and water and bring to boil in a saucepan. Add chicken and pork and simmer for 15 minutes. Add all other ingredients except cornstarch and water; simmer 5 minutes longer. Combine cornstarch and water, add to soup and stir until thickened.

Shanghai Watercress Soup
(for 4)

3 cups chicken broth
½ tsp. fresh ginger, minced
1 tsp. soy sauce
1 tsp. sherry
½ tsp. white vinegar

½ tsp. sugar
⅓ cup lean pork, shredded
1 scallion, trimmed and shredded
salt to taste
1 bunch watercress

Wash watercress, remove and discard big stems, dry and cut into 2 inch lengths. Put broth in a saucepan, add ginger root, soy sauce, sherry, sugar and vinegar, bring to a boil. Add pork, reduce heat and simmer for 15 minutes. Add scallion, salt and watercress, stir and simmer for 3 minutes.

Braised Soy Fish

(for 3)

2 lbs. fish (large whiting, sea bass, weak fish)
1 tsp. salt
flour
1½ tsp. fresh ginger root, minced
2 scallions, minced
1 small clove garlic, minced
5 tbsp. oil
1 cup chicken broth
2 tbsp. soy sauce
2 tbsp. oyster sauce
2 tbsp. sherry
pinch of cayenne pepper

Have fish cleaned and carefully scaled, but left whole. Wipe and dry fish with paper towels, inside and out. With a sharp knife score both sides of fish with 2 diagonal cuts. Sprinkle with salt and let stand 15 minutes. Then dust lightly with flour.

Combine scallions, ginger, garlic, chicken broth, soy sauce, oyster sauce, sherry and cayenne pepper, heat and keep warm.

Heat oil in a heavy saucepan, until quite hot. Put fish into pan, fry quickly for one minute, turn it over carefully with a spatula; fry the other side one minute, reduce heat, turn again very carefully and fry each side 2 minutes more. Baste fish with oil while frying. Pour the broth mixture over fish, bring to a boil, cover and cook gently about 15 minutes, until fish is done.

Steamed Sea Bass
(for 4)

2½-3 lb. sea bass
1 tsp. salt
1 clove garlic, crushed
½ tsp. salt
2 thin slices fresh ginger root, minced

2 scallions, minced
3 tbsp. soy sauce
1½ tbsp. sherry
1 tsp. sugar
1 tbsp. oil

Leave head and tail on cleaned and scaled fish. Score both sides of fish with three diagonal cuts. Sprinkle with one teaspoon salt. Mash garlic with ½ teaspoon salt to a paste. Combine with all other ingredients, blend well. Put fish on a shallow serving dish, spread mixed sauce over the fish. Place dish in a steamer and steam for about 30 minutes or until fish is done.

Stir-fried Striped Bass
(for 4)

1½ lbs. bass filet, skinned
1 tbsp. cornstarch
1 tbsp. soy sauce
1 tbsp. sherry
½ tsp. salt
pinch of cayenne pepper
1 clove garlic, crushed
1 scallion, minced

½ tsp. fresh ginger, minced
½ cup fresh mushrooms, sliced
¼ cup bamboo shoots, sliced thin
¼ cup celery, sliced thin
½ cup chicken broth
1 tsp. vinegar
½ tsp. sugar
4 tbsp. oil

Cut filets against grain in ¼ inch thick strips. Combine cornstarch, soy sauce, sherry, salt, cayenne and garlic, pour over fish filets and coat them. Heat 2 tablespoons oil in a wok, add scallion and ginger, stir for a few seconds, add vegetables, stir-fry for one minute. Then add broth, vinegar and sugar, cover and simmer for 2 or 3 minutes. Remove vegetables and their liquid from pan and keep warm. Add remaining oil to wok, add fish and stir-fry for about 2 or 3 minutes. Be careful not to break the fish. Return vegetables and liquid to pan, stir, heat through and serve.

Braised Cod Fish Steaks
(for 4)

4 codfish steaks, 2½ inches
  thick
2 scallions, minced
1 small clove garlic, minced
1 tsp. ginger root, minced
2 tbsp. onion, minced
2 tbsp. sherry

1 tbsp. soy sauce
1 tbsp. oyster sauce
½ tsp. sugar
½ tsp. vinegar
½ cup chicken broth
4 tbsp. oil
1 tsp. salt

Heat oil in a saucepan. When quite hot, brown fish steaks quickly on both sides. Add all other ingredients, simmer covered for about 15 minutes, until fish is done.

Shrimp and Fish Balls
(for 4)

1 lb. filet of sole (or any
  fresh water fish)
6 shrimp, shelled and deveined
3 scallions

1 tbsp. cornstarch
½ tsp. sesame oil (opt.)
salt to taste
oil for deep frying

Mince fish, shrimp and scallions, combine with cornstarch, sesame oil and salt, mince until smooth or put in a food processor. Form into 1 inch balls and fry, a few at a time, in deep fat until golden brown, about 3 minutes.

Fried Shrimp
(for 3)

12 jumbo shrimp
1 large clove garlic
½ tsp. salt
1 tbsp. grated ginger root
1 cup flour, sifted
4½ tsp. baking powder

2 tbsp. cornstarch
6 tbsp. oil
1 cup water (approx.)
oil for deep frying
scallions, cut lengthwise in
   thin strips

Shell shrimp but leave the tail segment of the shell, butterfly shrimp and devein. Crush garlic with salt to a paste and rub into shrimp, sprinkle with a little ginger root.

Blend flour, baking powder, cornstarch; add oil gradually while stirring. Stir until mixture forms a ball. Add water, a little at a time, while stirring until the mixture has the consistency of pancake batter.

Heat oil, dip each shrimp into the batter and fry, two or three at a time, until golden brown. Drain before serving. Garnish with scallion strips.

Braised Shrimp
(for 4)

1 lb. large shrimp, shelled
   and deveined
3 tbsp. oil
2 tbsp. soy sauce
1½ tbsp. sherry
1 tsp. sugar

⅔ cup onion, sliced thin
1½ tsp. fresh ginger, minced
⅔ cup bamboo shoots,
   sliced lengthwise
2 tsp. cornstarch
¼ cup chicken broth

Cut shrimp in 1 inch pieces. Heat oil in wok, stir-fry shrimp for 1 minute; add soy sauce, sherry and sugar, stir well; add ginger, onion and bamboo shoots, fry 2 minutes until vegetables are softening. Cover and simmer 3 minutes. Blend cornstarch and broth, add to shrimp and stir to thicken.

Shrimp in Black Bean Sauce
(for 4)

2 tbsp. oil
1 lb. small shrimp, shelled and deveined
1 clove garlic, minced
1½ tbsp. fermented black beans, washed and crushed

1 tbsp. cornstarch
⅓ cup chicken broth
1 tbsp. sherry
1 tbsp. soy sauce
3 scallions, sliced

Heat oil in a wok, add shrimp and garlic, stir-fry for a minute or so until the shrimp just start to turn pink. Mix beans with chicken broth, add to the wok and stir until simmering, add scallions, cover and simmer for 2 minutes. Blend cornstarch, sherry and soy sauce, add to wok and stir to thicken.

Note: Fermented black beans are available in Chinese food stores.

Stir-fried Shrimp and Bean Sprouts
(for 4)

1 lb. small shrimp, shelled
and deveined
1 medium onion, shredded
2 scallions, cut in ½ inch
pieces
2 thin slices ginger root,
minced
1 small clove garlic, minced
½ cup bean sprouts, washed
and dried

1 tbsp. soy sauce
½ tsp. salt
¾ cup chicken broth
1½ tbsp. sherry
1 tsp. sugar
pinch of cayenne pepper
1 tbsp. cornstarch
2 tbsp. water
2½ tbsp. oil

Heat oil in a wok. Add ginger and stir-fry for 30 seconds. Add shrimp, onion, scallions and garlic and fry 1 minute. Add bean sprouts and stir-fry 1½ minutes. Combine soy sauce, salt, chicken broth, sherry, sugar and pepper, heat and add to wok. Stir and bring quickly to a boil. Dilute cornstarch in water, add to wok and stir to thicken.

Curried Shrimp
(for 4)

1 lb. medium shrimp
2 tbsp. oil
1 tsp. salt
1½ tbsp. curry powder
1 medium onion, sliced ¼ inch thick

1 tbsp. cornstarch
1 tbsp. water
1 tbsp. sherry
1 tsp. sugar
¾ cup chicken broth

Shell and devein shrimp. Heat oil and salt in a wok or skillet and stir-fry shrimp for 2 minutes. Remove shrimp and reserve. Clean wok and fry curry in dry wok over low heat for a few seconds. Then add onions and stir-fry for 30 seconds. Add shrimp and chicken broth, bring to a boil over high heat and cook, stirring, for 1 minute. Combine water, sherry, sugar and cornstarch, add to wok and cook for 1 minute until thickened.

Stir-fried Shrimp and Mushrooms
(for 4)

1 lb. medium shrimp, shelled and deveined

1 tbsp. cornstarch

3 tbsp. water

2 scallions, cut in 1 inch lengths

¼ lb. fresh mushrooms, sliced

1 stalk celery, white part, sliced very thin, 1 inch long

1 clove garlic, minced

2 tbsp. soy sauce

1½ tbsp. sherry

4 tbsp. oil

½ tsp. salt

Cut shrimp in half, dilute cornstarch in water, add to shrimp, toss to coat the shrimp pieces evenly. Heat 2 tablespoons oil in a wok, add scallions, stir-fry a few seconds, add mushrooms and celery, fry 2 minutes. Remove vegetables from pan and keep warm. Add remaining oil and salt to wok, heat, stir-fry shrimp for a minute or so, until the pieces start to turn pink. Mix garlic, sherry and soy sauce, add to the wok and blend with the shrimp. Return vegetables to pan, stir-fry 2 minutes.

Lobster Cantonese—See page 50 for recipe.→

Braised Soy Fish—See page 35 for recipe.→

Deep Fried Crabmeat and Fish Balls, Sweet and Sour
(for 4)

½ lb. fish filet (flounder, whiting or sole)
½ lb. lump crabmeat
2 scallions, minced
½ cup fresh mushrooms, minced
½ clove garlic, minced
1 tbsp. sherry
1 tsp. cornstarch

1 tbsp. soy sauce
1 tbsp. oyster sauce
1 pinch cayenne pepper
1 egg, beaten lightly
cornstarch
sweet and sour sauce
   (p. 154)
oil for deep frying

Mince fish, pick over crabmeat and mince. Combine fish, crabmeat, scallions, mushrooms, garlic, sherry, 1 teaspoon cornstarch, soy sauce, oyster sauce and cayenne. Shape into small balls, dip into beaten egg, coat lightly with cornstarch and deep fry until golden brown, 2 minutes or less. Drain on paper towel. Heat sweet and sour sauce, add crab balls to heat through.

←*Stir-fried Beef and Beans*—See page 81 for recipe.

Lobster Cantonese
(for 4)

2 lobsters (1½ lbs. each)
½ lb. lean pork, ground
3 tbsp. oil
½ cup chicken broth
1½ tbsp. cornstarch
2 tbsp. soy sauce
2 tbsp. sherry

1 tsp. salt
1 clove garlic, minced
1½ tsp. fresh ginger root,
   minced
2 scallions, minced
2 eggs, beaten
3 tbsp. water

Have the lobsters split and cleaned. Chop each in 1½ inch pieces and the claws in three pieces. Heat oil in a wok, add garlic and ginger, stir-fry a few seconds; add pork and scallions and fry 3 minutes until all traces of pink have disappeared. Add lobster, stir-fry 1 minute, stir in broth and salt, cover and cook gently for 3 minutes. Blend cornstarch with soy sauce and sherry, add to wok and stir to thicken. Beat eggs lightly and combine with water. Remove wok from heat and add eggs, stir until well mixed and serve.

Stir-fried Lobster Tails
and Mushrooms
(for 4)

4 lobster tails (about 1¼ lbs.)
1 tbsp. cornstarch
3 tbsp. water
1 tbsp. sherry
1 tsp. lemon juice
1 tsp. fresh ginger, minced
¼ lb. fresh mushrooms, sliced
3 scallions,
   sliced in 1 inch pieces

1 stalk celery,
   white part, minced
1 clove garlic, minced
2 tbsp. soy sauce
1 tbsp. sherry
1 tsp. sugar
5 tbsp. oil
1 tsp. salt

Cut lobster tails in 1½ inch cubes or slices. Combine cornstarch with water, ginger, 1 tablespoon sherry and 1 teaspoon lemon juice. Coat lobster tail pieces with this mixture.

Heat 2 tablespoons oil in a wok, add scallions, stir-fry a few seconds, add mushrooms, celery and garlic and fry 2 to 3 minutes. Remove vegetables from wok and keep warm.

Add remaining oil, heat and add salt and lobster pieces. Stir-fry rapidly until lobster starts to firm, about 2 to 3 minutes. Stir in the 2 tablespoons soy sauce, mixed with sherry and sugar, blend well. Return vegetables to wok, heat through and serve.

Lobster and Pork
(for 4)

2 lb. lobster
1 cup lean pork, minced
1 large clove garlic, minced
1 scallion, chopped
1 thin slice ginger root, minced
2 tbsp. soy sauce
1½ tbsp. sherry

½ tsp. sugar
pinch of cayenne pepper
½ tsp. salt
4 tbsp. oil
4 tbsp. chicken broth
1 tbsp. cornstarch
2 tbsp. water
1 egg, lightly beaten

Split live lobster (or have your fish man do it). Cut tail crosswise in 3 or 4 pieces. Chop claws into pieces. Reserve coral, if any, and tomalley. Blend garlic, ginger, scallion, soy sauce, sherry, pepper, sugar and salt. Blend with minced pork. Heat oil in a wok, add lobster pieces and stir-fry for 2 or 3 minutes until the pieces are bright red and the lobster meat white and firm. Remove lobster, keep warm. Add pork mixture to wok and stir-fry for 2 minutes until pork has lost any tinge of pink. Return lobster to wok, add the mashed coral and tomalley and chicken broth and heat to boiling. Dilute cornstarch in water and add to wok, stir until thickened. Add lightly beaten egg and stir for half a minute.

Braised Chicken Breast
(for 4)

2 chicken breasts, skinned, boned, cut in 2 inch squares
1 tbsp. cornstarch
1 tbsp. soy sauce
1 tbsp. sherry
½ tsp. salt
½ tsp. sugar
½ clove garlic, minced
1 thin slice ginger root, minced

⅓ cup green pepper, diced
½ cup fresh mushrooms, sliced
1 stalk celery, white part, diced
⅓ cup onion, sliced thin
¾ cup chicken broth
2 tbsp. soy sauce
1 tbsp. cornstarch
2 tbsp. water
2 tbsp. oil

Combine 1 tablespoon cornstarch, soy sauce, sherry, salt and sugar, add to chicken and coat the pieces. Let stand 15 minutes. Heat oil in a wok, add garlic and ginger root and stir-fry a few seconds. Add chicken and fry for a minute or so, then add chicken broth and soy sauce, stir, cover and simmer for 5 minutes. Add vegetables, cover again and sim-mer 15 minutes. Combine cornstarch and water, stir into pan to thicken

Steamed Chicken Breast
(for 4)

2 whole chicken breasts,
  boned and skinned
½ cup bamboo shoots
8 water chestnuts
6 Chinese mushrooms
2 tbsp. oil

1 tsp. sugar
1 tbsp. soy sauce
1 tbsp. sherry
salt and pepper to taste
2 tsp. cornstarch
1 tbsp. water

Cut chicken into 1½ inch cubes. Soak mushrooms in warm water for ½ hour, drain, discard stems and slice caps. Slice bamboo shoots and water chestnuts ⅛ inch thick. Blend oil, sugar, soy sauce, sherry, salt, pepper, cornstarch, and water. Blend well with all other ingredients. Put in serving dishes. Place in steamer and cook for 15 minutes.

Steamed Chicken Breast and Ham
(for 4)

2 whole chicken breasts, boned
3 slices smoked ham, ¼ inch
  thick
6 Chinese mushrooms

salt and pepper to taste
3 scallions
1 tbsp. oil
1½ tbsp. sherry

Do not skin the chicken breasts. Cut them crosswise into ½ inch thick slices. Cut ham into similar slices. Soak mushrooms in warm water for 30 minutes. Remove and discard stems, squeeze caps dry and cut them in half. Slice scallions lengthwise in half and then cut into 1½ inch long pieces. Sprinkle chicken with salt, pepper and oil; sprinkle ham slices with sherry. In a shallow, heatproof serving bowl arrange alternate layers of chicken — skin side up — and ham slices. Place mushrooms around the meat, sprinkle top with scallions. Steam for about 30 minutes or until cooked.

Chicken and Peaches Cantonese
(for 6)

2 whole skinned and boned
chicken breasts (about 1 lb.)
1½ tsp. salt
¼ tsp. pepper
1½ tbsp. oil
1 large onion, sliced
1 cup catsup

1 can (16 ounces) sliced
peaches (drain; reserve syrup)
2 tbsp. soy sauce
1 large green pepper, cut
in squares
3 cups hot cooked rice

Cut chicken in thin strips, sprinkle with salt and pepper, stir-fry in oil about 2 minutes. Add onion, continue cooking until onion is tender crisp. Blend catsup, peach syrup with enough water to make two cups liquid, and soy sauce. Pour over chicken. Cover and simmer 20 minutes. Add green pepper and peaches. Replace cover and continue cooking 10 minutes longer. Serve over beds of rice.

Chicken and Cashew Nuts
(for 4)

2 whole chicken breasts,
  skinned and boned
1½ tbsp. cornstarch
3 tbsp. sherry
3 thin slices, ginger root,
  minced
2 stalks celery, white part
  only, minced
3 scallions, cut in ¼ inch
  lengths
⅓ cup onions, chopped

1 clove garlic, minced
4 tbsp. soy sauce
2 tbsp. sherry
1½ tsp. sesame oil
2 tsp. sugar
⅓ cup chicken broth
4 tbsp. oil
⅓ cup roasted cashew nuts
2 tsp. cornstarch
1½ tbsp. water

Cut chicken breast in medium cubes. Put the cubes in a bowl and mix them with the combined 1½ tablespoons cornstarch and 3 tablespoons sherry. Heat 3 tablespoons oil in a wok and stir-fry chicken cubes for about 3 minutes until chicken takes on color. Remove chicken and keep warm. Add remaining oil to wok, combine ginger, celery, scallions, onion and garlic and stir-fry for 2 minutes. Add cashews, stir for a few seconds. Return chicken to wok, add combined soy sauce, sherry, sesame oil, broth and sugar and stir until heated through. Dilute cornstarch with water, add to wok and stir until thickened.

Cantonese Stir-fried Chicken

(for 4)

2 whole chicken breasts, boned and skinned
3 tbsp. oil
½ tsp. salt
4 scallions, minced
6 firm fresh mushroom caps, sliced

1 cup bamboo shoots, shredded
¾ cup chicken broth
1½ tbsp. soy sauce
1 tbsp. sherry
1 tsp. sugar
1½ tbsp. cornstarch
4 tbsp. water

Shred chicken breasts. Heat 2 tablespoons oil and salt in a wok, add chicken and stir-fry until all traces of pink have disappeared. Remove chicken from wok and keep warm. Add remaining oil, heat and stir-fry scallions, bamboo shoots and mushrooms for 2 minutes. Return chicken to wok, add broth, soy sauce, sherry and sugar, cover and simmer for 2 minutes. Add cornstarch diluted in water, stir until thickened.

Stir-fried Chicken and Vegetables
(for 4)

1 chicken breast
2 chicken thighs
1 clove garlic, minced
1 slice fresh ginger root, minced
½ cup fresh mushrooms, sliced
¼ cup celery, white part, diced
½ green pepper, seeded, diced
½ cup bamboo shoots, diced

1 small leek, white part, sliced thin
1 small onion, sliced thin
2½ tbsp. oil
1 tsp. salt
½ cup chicken broth
1 tbsp. soy sauce
2 tsp. cornstarch
2 tbsp. sherry

Skin and bone chicken and dice. Heat 1½ tablespoons oil in a wok, add salt and stir. Add garlic and ginger, stir-fry a few seconds, add vegetables and fry 2 minutes. Add chicken broth and soy sauce, bring to a boil, cover and simmer 2 minutes. Remove vegetables and liquid from wok and keep warm. Add remaining oil to wok, heat and stir-fry chicken for 2 minutes. Return vegetables and liquid to pan, blend, cook for one minute until hot, stir in cornstarch blended with sherry and stir to thicken.

Chicken and Mushrooms
(for 4)

2 whole chicken breasts, boned and skinned
1 tsp. salt
pinch of cayenne pepper
1 tbsp. cornstarch
3 tbsp. oil
2 thin slices ginger root, minced

1½ cups very small fresh button mushrooms
1 small green pepper
2 scallions, chopped
1 tbsp. cornstarch
3 tbsp. chicken broth
1 tbsp. sherry

Cut chicken breasts into small cubes. Put them in a bowl and mix with salt, cayenne and 1 tablespoon cornstarch. Heat oil in a wok, add ginger and stir-fry for 30 seconds. Add chicken and fry until all traces of pink have disappeared, about 2½ minutes. Remove chicken from wok and keep warm. Stir-fry mushrooms, green pepper, seeded and cut into ¼ inch strips, and scallions for 2 minutes. Return chicken to wok, heat through. Dilute cornstarch in broth and sherry, add to wok and stir until thickened.

Red Simmered Chicken
(for 4)

3 lb. frying chicken
1 clove garlic, crushed
3 thin slices fresh ginger
  root, minced
2 scallions, chopped
2 tsp. brown sugar

2 tbsp. sherry
1 clove star anise
$^1/_3$ cup soy sauce
½ cup chicken broth
2 tsp. sesame oil

Wash chicken, inside and out, dry well with paper towels and truss. Put all other ingredients in a heavy saucepan, mix and bring to a boil. Add chicken, reduce heat, cover and simmer for an hour or until chicken is cooked. Turn chicken three or four times while cooking. To serve, bone chicken and coat meat with sauce.

Stir-fried Chicken, Pork and Pineapple

(for 4)

1 chicken breast, boned, skinned, sliced thin
1/3 lb. lean pork, sliced thin
2 tsp. cornstarch
1 tsp. sherry
1 tsp. water
3/4 cup canned pineapple chunks
1 clove garlic, minced

1 tsp. fresh ginger, minced
2 tsp. cornstarch
1 tbsp. soy sauce
1 tbsp. sherry
1 tbsp. hoisin sauce
¼ cup pineapple juice
1 tsp. lemon juice
3 tbsp. oil

Combine cornstarch, 1 teaspoon sherry and 1 teaspoon water, coat chicken and pork slices with the mixture.

Heat oil in a wok, add pork and stir-fry for one minute, add chicken and fry two minutes more. Add pineapple, cover and cook for 3 minutes then remove meat and pineapple and keep hot. Combine garlic, ginger, cornstarch, soy sauce, sherry, hoisin sauce, pineapple juice and lemon juice, add to wok, stir until sauce thickens and is hot. Pour over meat and serve.

Honey Chicken
(for 4)

3 lb. frying chicken cut in serving pieces
½ cup sherry
2 tbsp. soy sauce
2 tbsp. honey
1 tsp. vinegar
salt to taste

1 tsp. fresh ginger, shredded
2 scallions, white part only, chopped
1 clove garlic, minced
2 tbsp. oil
1 tbsp. cornstarch

Heat oil in a saucepan, saute chicken pieces until well browned on all sides. Remove chicken, pour off oil from pan. Combine all other ingredients except cornstarch, add to pan, stir well and let come to a simmer. Return chicken to pan, cover and simmer for about 45 minutes. Five minutes before chicken is done, dilute cornstarch with a little water, add to pan and stir until thickened.

Chicken Wings in Oyster Sauce
(for 4)

8 chicken wings
6 thin slices ginger root
1 large clove garlic, mashed
$^1/_3$ cup chicken broth
4 tbsp. oyster sauce

2 tbsp. soy sauce
½ tsp. vinegar
3 tbsp. sherry
1 tbsp. oil
½ tsp. salt

Cut chicken wings in three pieces and discard wing tips. Heat oil and salt in a wok or skillet over medium heat and stir-fry ginger and garlic until browned. Discard ginger and garlic, add wings and all other ingredients, bring to a boil and simmer covered for 30 minutes. Turn the wings once in a while. Add more broth if needed.

Stir-fried Chicken Livers
(for 4)

1 lb. chicken livers
½ cup bamboo shoots, sliced
4 water chestnuts, sliced thin
2 thin slices fresh ginger
   root, shredded
⅓ cup snowpeas (opt.)

4 Chinese mushrooms
4 tbsp. oil
½ tsp. salt
½ tsp. sugar
1½ tbsp. soy sauce
1½ tbsp. sherry

Wash livers, pat dry and cut each in half. Soak mushrooms in warm water for 20 minutes, discard stem, squeeze dry and slice caps. Heat 1½ tablespoons oil in a wok, stir-fry mushrooms for one minute; add bamboo shoots and water chestnuts, stir-fry one minute; add snowpeas and fry one minute longer. Remove vegetables and keep warm. Add remaining oil to wok, heat, add salt and sugar, ginger and livers. Stir-fry over high heat for about 2 minutes. Stir in soy sauce and sherry, return vegetables to wok, stir until well heated.

Stir-fried Chicken Livers
and Mushrooms
(for 4)

¾ lb. chicken livers
2 tsp. cornstarch
1 tbsp. soy sauce
1 tbsp. sherry
1 small clove garlic, crushed
2 dashes tabasco sauce
½ lb. fresh mushrooms, sliced
very thin

1 small onion, slivered
2 water chestnuts, shredded
2 scallions, white part
only, chopped
¼ tsp. cracked black pepper
4 tbsp. oil
4 tbsp. chicken broth

Trim livers and cut in half. Combine 2 teaspoons cornstarch, soy sauce, sherry, garlic and tabasco, pour over livers, mix and let stand 15 minutes. Heat 2 tablespoons oil, add onion and scallions, stir-fry a few seconds, add other vegetables and fry about 2 minutes. Remove vegetables and keep warm.

Add remaining oil to pan, heat, add livers and pepper and stir-fry quickly for about 2 minutes, return vegetables to pan, heat through, stir in chicken broth and serve.

Sweet and Sour Chicken Livers
(for 4)

¾ lb. chicken livers
2 tsp. cornstarch
1 tbsp. sherry
1 pinch cayenne pepper
1 tbsp. soy sauce
1 small clove garlic, minced

½ tsp. fresh ginger, minced
1 scallion, white part
  only, minced
2 tbsp. oil
½ tsp. salt
sweet and sour sauce

Trim livers and cut in half. Pour boiling water over them and let stand ½ minute and drain. Combine cornstarch, sherry, pepper and soy sauce, pour over livers and toss. Heat oil in a wok. Add salt, garlic, scallion, and ginger, stir-fry a few seconds, then add livers and fry over fairly high heat for 2 minutes. Add sweet and sour sauce, reduce heat and stir-fry a couple of minutes longer.

Braised Duck
(for 4-5)

1 duck (5 lbs.)
1 tbsp. soy sauce
1 tbsp. sherry
1 tsp. cornstarch
1 clove garlic, mashed
1 tbsp. hoisin sauce
2 tbsp. oil
3 scallions, chopped
2 thin slices fresh ginger
  root, minced
½ cup onion, sliced thin

1 clove garlic, chopped
1 tsp. sugar
3 tbsp. soy sauce
2 tbsp. sherry
2 cups chicken broth
1 cup water
½ cup celery, sliced
½ cup water chestnuts, diced
1 tbsp. cornstarch
2 tbsp. water

Wipe duck with a damp cloth, cut in quarters or smaller pieces. Blend soy sauce, sherry, cornstarch, mashed garlic and hoisin sauce, rub into duck pieces and let stand for an hour. Heat oil in a heavy saucepan, brown the duck pieces on all sides. Remove duck and drain off all fat. Add scallions, ginger, onion and garlic, stir-fry for a few seconds, return duck to pan, add sugar, soy sauce, sherry, chicken broth and water, cover and simmer for about one hour or until duck is cooked. Half an hour after starting to simmer the duck, add celery and water chestnuts. When duck is cooked, remove to hot platter, skim fat off the sauce, add cornstarch diluted in water and stir to thicken.

Spiced Roast Duck
(for 4)

5 lb. Long Island duck
2 tbsp. salt
2 tbsp. sherry
2 tbsp. hoisin sauce

¼ tsp. dry mustard
¾ tsp. ground allspice
2 tbsp. dark corn syrup
1 tbsp. Bovril or other
beef extract

Wipe duck inside and out with a damp cloth. Dry thoroughly with paper towels. Rub inside and out with salt and let stand uncovered in the refrigerator overnight. Blend sherry and all other ingredients. Rub this sauce with your hand on the duck, inside and out. Let duck stand for 3 hours at room temperature. Pour water, one inch deep, in a roasting pan. Place a rack in the pan and put the duck, breast side up, on the rack above the water. Roast duck for one hour in a preheated 300⁰ oven. Then turn duck breast side down and roast for another hour. Turn duck breast side up again, increase heat to 350⁰ and roast 30 minutes longer. Remove from oven and let cool. Cut into bite size pieces before serving.

Roast Duck Cantonese
(for 6)

1 duck (5 lbs.)
salt
1 large clove garlic, minced
1½ tsp. minced fresh
    ginger root
2 scallions, minced
2 tbsp. soy sauce

2 tbsp. sherry
1 cup chicken broth
¼ tsp. allspice
3 tbsp. honey
2 tbsp. soy sauce
1 tbsp. vinegar
½ cup chicken broth

Wipe the duck, inside and out, with a damp cloth, then dry with paper towels. Rub the duck lightly, inside and out, with salt. Let stand for 15 minutes, then dry again. Combine garlic, ginger, scallions, 2 tablespoons soy sauce, sherry, chicken broth and allspice in a saucepan. Let come to a boil, take off heat and cool slightly. Sew up the neck cavity of the duck to make it as leakproof as possible. Stand duck, neck down, in a bowl and pour the hot liquid in the cavity. Truss the opening tightly. Place duck on a rack in a roasting pan, cover bottom with an inch or so of water. Put duck in a preheated 375⁰ oven for 20 minutes. Combine remaining soy sauce, honey, vinegar and chicken broth. Reduce heat to 325⁰ and roast duck 1½ hours, basting every 15 minutes with the honey mixture. When done, remove from oven, let stand 10 minutes, then remove skewers and let liquid run from cavity into a bowl. Carve and spoon the sauce over the portions.

Roast Aromatic Duck
(for 6)

1 duck (5 lbs.)
1 clove garlic, mashed
2 scallions, minced
2 thin slices fresh ginger
    root, minced
1/3 cup soy sauce
2 tbsp. honey

2 tbsp. sherry
1 tsp. vinegar
1 tsp. salt
1 pinch allspice
1 orange
1/2 cup dry white wine
oil

Wipe duck inside and out with a damp cloth. Combine all ingredients except orange and sherry. Pour half of the mixture into the duck cavity, cover all the inner surface, then place the orange in the cavity and close the opening with skewers and string. Rub the remaining mixture into the duck skin and let stand for an hour. Place duck on a rack in a roasting pan and add an inch or so of water to the pan. Roast in preheated 325⁰ oven for 2 hours. Brush a few times with oil during roasting. After 2 hours, remove all liquid from roasting pan and reserve. Remove rack and put duck back into the pan, sprinkle sherry over the duck and roast 30 minutes longer. Skim fat off the liquid removed from the pan, reduce to thicken a bit, and pour over the bird before serving.

Stir-fried Duck and Vegetables
(for 4)

1 cup bamboo shoots
12 medium fresh mushroom caps
¾ cup cooked duck meat
2 tbsp. oil
1 tbsp. sherry

1 tbsp. water
1 tbsp. oyster sauce
1 tbsp. cornstarch
salt

Dice bamboo shoots, mushrooms and skinless duck meat into approximately ½ inch cubes. Blend sherry, water, oyster sauce and cornstarch. Heat oil in a wok until very hot, add the salt. Add mushrooms and bamboo shoots and stir-fry for 3 minutes. Add duck and fry one more minute, then add the sherry mixture and cook one minute longer.

Stir-fried Curried Pork—See page 95 for recipe.→

Assorted Spices.→

Stir-fried Duck
(for 4)

1 duck (5 lbs.)
2 tsp. cornstarch
1 tbsp. soy sauce
1 tbsp. sherry
1 tsp. honey
1 small clove garlic, minced
½ tsp. ginger root, minced

3 tbsp. oil
2 scallions, sliced
½ cup bamboo shoots, diced
½ cup celery, diced
½ cup chicken broth
pepper and salt to taste

Bone duck breast and legs (or ask your butcher to do it), cut meat in 1 inch cubes. Combine cornstarch, soy sauce, sherry, honey, garlic and ginger root, coat duck meat with the mixture and let stand for 30 minutes. Heat 1½ tablespoons of oil in a wok, stir-fry duck until lightly browned, about 3 minutes. Remove duck from pan, drain off all fat. Add remaining oil, heat and stir-fry scallions, bamboo shoots and celery for 3 minutes. Return duck to pan, add broth, salt and pepper, cover and cook for about 5 minutes, until duck is cooked.

←*Chicken and Peaches Cantonese*—See page 56 for recipe.

Braised Squab and Mushrooms

(for 4)

2 squabs
2 tbsp. soy sauce
2 tbsp. sherry
1 clove garlic, mashed
¼ lb. smoked ham
  (½ cup) diced
2 tbsp. sherry

¼ tsp. allspice
1 tsp. minced fresh ginger
½ lb. fresh button mushrooms
1 tbsp. soy sauce
2 tbsp. oil
2 scallions sliced lengthwise

Quarter squabs and wipe with a damp cloth. Combine 2 tablespoons soy sauce, 2 tablespoons sherry and garlic, rub the pieces of squab with the mixture and let stand for 15 minutes.

Heat oil in heavy pan, brown squab on all sides. Add all other ingredients except mushrooms and scallions, cover and simmer for 30 minutes. Add mushrooms and continue simmering for another 30 minutes, until meat is tender. Put on serving platter and garnish with scallion strips.

Chinese Steak

(for 6)

1 flank steak, 2 to 2½ lbs.
2 tbsp. oil
⅓ cup soy sauce
2 tbsp. honey
1 clove garlic, mashed

3 tbsp. sherry
½ tsp. powdered ginger
  root
1 tsp. hot mustard
pepper to taste

Trim the steak and score the surface in a diamond pattern. Blend all other ingredients. Put steak in a shallow pan, pour the soy sauce mixture over it, coat the steak on both sides with the mixture. Let stand for 4 to 6 hours, turning it once in a while.

Broil under a very hot broiler or over charcoal. Cut into very thin slices when serving.

Stir-fried Beef and Nuts
(for 4)

1 lb. flank steak
1 tsp. sugar
2 tsp. cornstarch
1 tbsp. soy sauce
1 tbsp. sherry
4 tbsp. oil
¾ cup beef broth

2 tbsp. soy sauce
1 tsp. sesame oil
⅓ cup onion, coarsely chopped
2 scallions, chopped
½ cup cashew nuts
1½ tbsp. cornstarch
3 tbsp. water

Cut meat across grain into 2 inch long slices, ¼ inch wide. Put beef in a bowl and mix well with 2 teaspoons cornstarch, 1 tablespoon soy sauce, sugar and sherry. Heat 3 tablespoons oil in a wok and stir-fry beef for 2½ minutes until all traces of red have disappeared. Remove beef and keep warm. Add remaining oil to wok, heat, add onion and stir-fry for not quite a minute. Add scallions and fry half a minute longer. Return beef to wok, add nuts and stir-fry half a minute. Combine broth, 2 tablespoons soy sauce and sesame oil, add to meat and stir-fry 2 minutes. Dilute cornstarch with water, add to meat and stir until it thickens.

Stir-fried Beef and Beans
(for 4)

¾ lb. flank steak

1 tbsp. cornstarch

1 tbsp. sherry

2 tbsp. soy sauce

¾ tsp. sugar

½ tsp. salt

¾ lb. string beans, trimmed, cut in long strips

1 small clove garlic, minced

4 tbsp. oil

½ cup beef broth

Slice beef across the grain in thin slices. Mix cornstarch, sherry, soy sauce, and sugar, add to beef and toss to coat the slices. Parboil string beans for a minute, drain and cool. Heat 2 tablespoons oil in a wok, add garlic, stir-fry a few seconds, add beef and stir-fry a couple of minutes until lightly browned. Remove beef from pan and reserve. Add remaining oil to wok, add salt, heat and add string beans. Fry a minute, add broth, heat to a boil, return beef, cover and simmer for 2 minutes.

Stir-fried Beef in Oyster Sauce

(for 4)

1 lb. flank steak
2 tsp. cornstarch
2 tsp. water
½ tsp. white vinegar
1 tsp. sugar
1 thin slice fresh ginger root
3 tbsp. oil

3 scallions, minced
3 tbsp. oyster sauce
⅔ cup chicken broth
2 tbsp. sherry
1 tbsp. cornstarch
1½ tbsp. water

Slice meat across grain ¼ inch wide and 2 inches long. Put meat in a bowl and mix with sugar, 2 teaspoons cornstarch and 2 teaspoons water and vinegar. Heat oil in wok, add ginger root and stir-fry for one minute until lightly browned. Discard ginger root, add beef slices and stir-fry for two minutes until all traces of red have disappeared. Add scallions and stir-fry for half a minute longer. Stir in the combined oyster sauce, chicken broth and sherry, fry for a minute or more until bubbling. Dilute cornstarch with water, add to wok and stir until thickened.

Stir-fried Beef and Scallions
(for 4)

1 lb. flank steak
(or sirloin)
3 tbsp. oil
½ tsp. salt
8 scallions, cut diagonally
into 1 inch pieces
1 clove garlic, minced

6 very thin slices fresh
ginger root
½ cup chicken broth
2 tsp. soy sauce
1 tbsp. cornstarch
1½ tbsp. water

Cut beef across grain into ¼ inch thick slices. Heat oil in a wok, add salt and stir-fry for half a minute. Add scallions, garlic and ginger root cut in strips, fry for 1 minute. Add meat and stir-fry about 3 minutes until all traces of red have disappeared. Add broth and soy sauce, fry another minute or so. Dilute cornstarch with water, add to wok and stir until sauce thickens.

Stir-fried Beef in Black Bean Sauce

(for 4)

1 lb. flank steak
2 tbsp. fermented black beans
2 medium sweet red peppers
(or green if red ones
not available)
1 medium onion
4 tbsp. oil

3 thin slices fresh ginger
root
1 clove garlic, crushed
2 tbsp. sherry
1 tsp. soy sauce
1½ tbsp. cornstarch
²/₃ cup beef broth

Slice beef across grain into 2 inch squares. Soak beans in water for 10 minutes, drain and mash with a fork. Remove seeds and membranes of peppers, cut into 1 inch diamonds. Slice and cut onion into strips. Heat 3 tablespoons of oil in a wok, add ginger root and garlic, stir-fry for a minute. Remove and discard garlic. Add beef and stir-fry for 3 minutes. Remove beef and keep warm. Add remaining oil, heat and add pepper and onion and fry for 2 minutes. Remove vegetables from pan and keep warm. Add black beans to wok, stir for half a minute, then add beef broth and bring to a boil. Mix sherry, soy sauce and cornstarch. Return meat and vegetables to wok and heat through. Add cornstarch mixture and stir until thickened.

Stir-fried Beef and Bok Choy
(for 4)

1 lb. flank steak
2 cups Chinese cabbage, sliced
1 clove garlic, mashed
2 thin slices ginger root, minced
3 scallions
¼ cup beef broth

1 tbsp. soy sauce
1 tbsp. sherry
pepper to taste
2 tsp. cornstarch
3 tbsp. water
2 tbsp. oil

Cut cabbage at a slant into ¼ inch slices. Cut flank steak across the grain into ¼ inch thick slices, 2 inches long. Slice scallions lengthwise in half and then cut into 2 inch pieces. Heat one tablespoon oil in a wok, add ginger and garlic and stir-fry for a minute until starting to brown. Add cabbage and scallions, fry for another minute or two. Combine beef broth, soy sauce, sherry and pepper, add to wok, blend and cover. Cook for a minute. Remove vegetables and sauce from wok and reserve. Clean wok, heat 1 tablespoon oil and stir-fry beef over high flame for 1 minute. Add reserved vegetables and sauce and heat through. Dilute cornstarch in water, add to the pan and stir for a minute until thickened.

Stir-fried Shredded Beef
(for 3)

¾ lb. flank steak, shredded
2 tbsp. soy sauce
1 tsp. sherry
1 tsp. hoisin sauce
1 small clove garlic, minced
1 slice fresh ginger, shredded
2 scallions, chopped

1 cup shredded celery
¼ cup shredded bamboo shoots
½ cup shredded carrot
3 tbsp. oil
½ tsp. dried red
(hot) pepper

Add soy sauce, sherry, hoisin sauce and garlic to beef, mix well. Heat 1½ tablespoons oil in a wok, add beef and stir-fry about 2 minutes until it starts to turn brown. Remove beef from wok and keep warm. Add remaining oil to wok. Heat, add ginger root, stir for a few seconds, add scallions and carrots, stir-fry 1 minute. Add bamboo shoots, celery and red pepper, fry 1 minute more. Return beef, stir to heat through.

Stir-fried Steak and Onions
(for 4)

1 lb. flank steak, sliced
2 tbsp. sherry
2 tbsp. oyster sauce
1 tbsp. cornstarch

4 tbsp. oil
3 medium onions, sliced
1 tsp. sugar
1 tsp. salt

Combine sherry, oyster sauce and cornstarch, marinate steak slices in this mixture for 15 minutes. Heat 1 tablespoon oil in a wok or skillet, stir-fry onions until wilted. Add sugar and salt, stir, then remove onions from wok and reserve. Add remaining oil to wok, stir-fry the meat for 4 minutes, return the onions to wok, heat through quickly, and serve.

Green Pepper Steak
(for 3)

¾ lb. flank steak
1 tsp. cornstarch
1 tsp. soy sauce
2 tsp. sherry
½ tsp. oil
½ tsp. sugar
2 green peppers
1 large clove garlic, minced
1 tbsp. fermented black
  beans (opt.)

1 slice fresh ginger root,
  minced
1 medium onion
1 tbsp. soy sauce
2 tbsp. cornstarch
1 pinch sugar
⅛ tsp. black pepper
1 dash tabasco sauce
salt to taste
3 tbsp. oil

Slice trimmed steak across the grain into ¼ inch slices, 2 inches long. Blend sherry, soy sauce, 1 tablespoon cornstarch, ½ teaspoon sugar and ½ teaspoon oil. Coat the sliced meat with this mixture and marinate for 15 minutes. Cut peppers in half, remove membranes and seeds and cut into ¼ inch wide strips. Slice onion ¼ inch thick and then into 1 inch strips. Mix soy sauce, cornstarch, pinch of sugar, pepper, tabasco and salt. Heat 1½ tablespoons oil in a wok. Stir-fry beef over high heat for one minute. Remove beef and reserve. Clean wok. Heat the other 1½ tablespoons oil. Add garlic, ginger root and the mashed black beans, stir-fry one minute, add green pepper and onion, stir-fry for 2 minutes. Return beef to wok, add the cornstarch mixture and cook, stirring for another minute until the sauce thickens.

Braised Beef and Vegetables
(for 6)

2 lbs. round or shoulder beef
1 clove garlic, minced
2 scallions, minced
1 slice fresh ginger root,
   minced
¼ tsp. allspice
4 tbsp. soy sauce
3 tbsp. sherry

1 tbsp. vinegar
salt and pepper to taste
3 tbsp. oil
2 cups beef broth
1 cup shelled green peas
½ cup bamboo shoots, diced
2 stalks celery, white part,
   sliced thin

Heat oil in a heavy saucepan, stir in garlic, add beef and brown quickly on all sides. Blend scallions, ginger, allspice, soy sauce, sherry, vinegar, salt and pepper, add to meat, stir and turn the meat in the combined ingredients. Heat gently. In the meantime bring beef broth to a boil, pour over beef, bring to a boil again, cover the pan and simmer for about 1½ hours or until beef is tender. Fifteen minutes before the beef is done, add the vegetables, cover again and continue cooking.

Red Simmered Beef
(for 6)

2½ lbs. sirloin tip or eye
  round
3 tbsp. oil
2 thin slices fresh ginger
  root
1 clove garlic, crushed
5 tbsp. soy sauce

5 tbsp. sherry
water
chicken broth
2 cloves star anise
⅛ tsp. cinnamon
salt and pepper to taste
2 tsp. brown sugar

Have butcher tie the meat so that it will keep its shape during cooking. Heat oil in a heavy casserole. Brown beef on all sides. Add half water and half broth, just enough to cover the meat. Add and mix in all other ingredients. Reduce heat and cook gently for about 1½ hours, until meat is done. Turn the meat once in a while during cooking. Slice and serve with the sauce.

Sweet and Sour Beef Balls
(for 4)

1 lb. lean beef
2 tbsp. onion, minced
1 tsp. fresh ginger root, minced
1 small clove garlic, minced
1 egg
1 tbsp. flour
salt to taste

1½ cups beef broth
2 tbsp. brown sugar
3 tbsp. soy sauce
4 tbsp. vinegar
pinch of cayenne pepper
2 tsp. cornstarch
1 tbsp. water

Grind beef very fine or mince with sharp knives. Blend with onion, ginger, garlic, the lightly beaten egg and flour. Do not handle too much. Shape into small balls. Bring broth to a boil in a deep, smallish saucepan. Drop beef balls, a few at a time into the broth and simmer, covered, until done. Remove them as they get done and keep hot. When all are cooked, add sugar, soy sauce, vinegar, salt and cayenne to the broth, stir well. Blend cornstarch and water, stir into broth to thicken and pour over beef balls.

Beef Balls with Pineapple

(for 4)

1 lb. lean beef, ground
1 egg
1 tbsp. cornstarch
1 tsp. salt
2 tbsp. onion, minced
3 tbsp. oil
4 slices pineapple, cut
  into chunks
2 large green peppers, seeded
  and cut into long strips

For the sauce:

1 tbsp. oil
1 cup pineapple juice
3 tbsp. cornstarch
1 tbsp. soy sauce
3 tbsp. vinegar
6 tbsp. water
¼ cup brown sugar
½ tsp. dry mustard

First prepare the sauce. Combine all ingredients and cook, stirring until well blended, thickened and simmering. Keep warm.

Blend beef with lightly beaten egg, cornstarch, salt, onions, form about 12 to 16 balls, heat oil in wok and fry the balls for about 3 minutes, until browned. Drain on paper towel. Heat sauce, add beef balls, stir until heated through. Garnish with pineapple chunks and green pepper.

Basic Stir-fried Pork
(for 4)

1 lb. lean pork
1½ tbsp. cornstarch
1 tbsp. sherry
1 tbsp. soy sauce
4 cups vegetables
1 large clove garlic, crushed

4 tbsp. oil
2 thin slices fresh ginger, minced
⅓ cup chicken broth
2 tbsp. soy sauce
½ tsp. salt

Cut pork, across the grain, in thin slices. Dissolve cornstarch in sherry and soy sauce, add to pork, blend and let stand for 20 minutes. Slice vegetables into thin strips. Heat 2 tablespoons oil in a wok, add salt and heat. Add garlic and stir-fry a few seconds. Add pork and stir-fry pork about 3 minutes until all traces of pink have disappeared and it starts to brown lightly. Remove from wok and keep warm. Add remaining oil to wok and heat. Add ginger root and vegetables, stir-fry one minute. Mix chicken broth and 2 tablespoons soy sauce, add to wok, stir, cover and cook over medium flame, until vegetables are nearly done. Return pork, stir-fry uncovered over high heat for a minute or so, until blended and hot.

Note: There are any numbers of mixed vegetables that can be used. Bean sprouts, celery, carrots, bamboo shoots, water chestnuts, peppers, mushrooms, onions, string beans, and others, according to your taste.

Stir-fried Pork and Bean Sprouts

(for 4)

¾ lb. lean pork
1 lb. bean sprouts
1 thin slice fresh ginger
   root, minced
1 clove garlic, mashed
1 tbsp. sherry

1 tbsp. soy sauce
½ tsp. sugar
3 tbsp. oil
½ tsp. salt
1 tbsp. hoisin sauce

Wash bean sprouts, blanch in boiling water, drain and cool. Cut pork across the grain in thin strips. Blend ginger, garlic, sherry, soy sauce and sugar, pour over pork, mix and marinate for 15 minutes.

Heat 1½ tablespoons oil in a wok, add marinated pork and stir-fry for 3 minutes until all traces of pink have disappeared. Remove pork and keep warm. Add remaining oil and salt to wok, heat well and stir-fry bean sprouts for ½ minutes, sprinkle with hoisin sauce and fry another minute. Return pork to wok, blend and stir-fry until hot.

Stir-fried Curried Pork

(for 4)

¾ lb. lean pork
1 medium onion, sliced thin
1 green pepper, sliced
1 clove garlic, mashed
½ tsp. ginger root, minced
2 tbsp. oil
½ tsp. salt

1½ tsp. curry powder
1 tbsp. sherry
1 tsp. lemon juice
⅓ cup chicken broth
2 tsp. cornstarch
1½ tbsp. water

Cut pork across grain in thin strips. Heat oil in a wok, add salt, stir-fry pork for 2 to 3 minutes until all traces of pink have disappeared. Add pepper, onion, garlic and ginger, stir-fry about 2 minutes or until vegetables have softened. Add curry powder and stir-fry 2 minutes over low heat. Add broth, sherry and lemon juice, mix well and fry 5 minutes over medium heat. Add cornstarch, diluted with water, and stir until thickened.

Stir-fried Pork in Oyster Sauce

(for 4)

¾ lb. lean pork
1½ tsp. cornstarch
1 tbsp. sherry
pinch of sugar
4 scallions, coarsely chopped
1 clove garlic, crushed
1 tsp. ginger root, minced

2 tsp. cornstarch
1 tbsp. water
2 tbsp. oyster sauce
2 tbsp. oil
½ tsp. salt
½ cup chicken broth

Slice pork against the grain in thin slices. Blend 1½ teaspoons cornstarch, sherry, sugar, add to pork, mix and let stand for 15 minutes. Heat oil and salt in a wok, add pork, garlic and ginger and stir-fry 3 minutes. Add scallions and fry 1 minute longer. Stir and blend in chicken broth. Blend 2 teaspoons cornstarch, water and oyster sauce, add to wok and stir to thicken.

Stir-fried Pork and Vegetables
(for 4)

4 dried Chinese mushrooms
²/₃ lb. lean pork
½ cup bamboo shoots
5 water chestnuts
3 scallions, trimmed
1 clove garlic, mashed
4 firm fresh mushroom caps
4 tbsp. oil

½ cup bean sprouts, washed and dried
1½ tbsp. sherry
salt and pepper to taste
½ cup chicken broth
1 tbsp. soy sauce
1 tbsp. cornstarch
3 tbsp. water

Soak mushrooms in hot water for ½ hour. Remove and discard stems and slice caps in strips. Slice pork across grain into ⅛ inch thick slices. Slice bamboo shoots and water chestnuts ¼ inch thick. Cut scallions diagonally into 1 inch pieces. Slice fresh mushrooms ¼ inch thick.

Put 2 tablespoons oil and salt in a wok and heat. Add garlic stir-fry 30 seconds, then remove and discard garlic. Add Chinese mushrooms, bamboo shoots, water chestnuts, and fresh mushrooms and stir-fry for one minute. Add bean sprouts and fry one minute longer. Remove vegetables from wok and reserve. Add remaining oil, heat, add scallions and stir-fry for half a minute, then add pork and fry 3 minutes. Stir in sherry and pepper. Return the vegetables, add chicken broth, soy sauce, bring to a boil and cook covered for 2 minutes. Then add the cornstarch dissolved in water and stir until the mixture thickens and serve.

Stir-fried Pork and Nuts

(for 4)

$^2/_3$ lb. lean pork
1 small celery heart
1 medium onion
8 medium carrots
1 small sweet red (or
  green) pepper
1 scallion, white part only
1½ tbsp. soy sauce
pinch of sugar
1 tbsp. cornstarch
4 tbsp. oil

pinch of salt
1 clove garlic, crushed
2 thin slices ginger
  roots, minced
$^1/_3$ cup cashew nuts
½ cup chicken broth
1 tbsp. soy sauce
1 tbsp. sherry
1 tsp. sesame oil
1 tbsp. cornstarch
3 tbsp. water

Slice pork across grain ¼ inch thick. Slice celery diagonally into 1½ inch lengths. Slice onion 1 inch thick and cut the slices in half. Peel and cut carrots diagonally in 1½ inch lengths. Cut pepper in half, remove membrane and seed, slice 2 inches long and ½ inch wide. Blend 1½ tablespoons soy sauce with sugar and 1 tablespoon cornstarch. Coat sliced pork with soy sauce mixture.

Cook carrots in boiling salt water for 4 minutes, drain and cool. Put 2 tablespoons oil and salt in a wok, heat and add pork. Stir-fry for 3 minutes until all traces of pink have disappeared. Remove pork and reserve. Add remaining oil and heat, then add ginger and garlic. Stir-fry for half a minute. Remove garlic and discard. Add all vegetables and cashew nuts and fry for 1½ minutes. Add broth, soy sauce, sherry and sesame oil, bring to a boil, cover and cook over moderate heat for 2½ minutes. Return pork to wok, heat through. Add cornstarch diluted with water, stir until it thickens.

Pork and Shrimp

(for 4)

¼ lb. lean loin of pork
(boneless weight)
¼ lb. ham
(Smithfield or similar)
8 medium raw shrimp, shelled
and deveined
3 Chinese mushrooms
2 water chestnuts
½ cup bamboo shoots

½ cup chicken broth
1 tbsp. hoisin sauce
2 tbsp. soy sauce
2 tsp. sugar
2 tsp. cornstarch
3 tbsp. water
¼ cup cashew nuts, halved
2 tbsp. oil

Dice pork, ham and bamboo shoots into ½ inch cubes. Soak mushrooms in warm water for half an hour, discard stems, drain and dice caps. Blend broth, hoisin sauce, soy sauce and sugar.

Heat oil in a wok or skillet until very hot. Add pork and stir-fry 2 minutes. Add shrimp and fry 1 minute. Add ham, bamboo shoots, mushrooms and cashew nuts and fry 2 minutes longer. Add the broth mixture, stir well, lower heat and cook covered for about 3 minutes. Dilute cornstarch with water, stir in to thicken.

Pork Balls

(for 4)

1 slice ginger root, minced

1 tbsp. scallion, white part only, minced

6 water chestnuts, minced

1 clove garlic, minced

1½ tbsp. cornstarch

1 tsp. sugar

¼ tsp. pepper

1 dash tabasco sauce

1 tbsp. soy sauce

2 tbsp. ketchup

1 lb. lean ground pork

oil for frying

Mix all ingredients, except oil, without handling too much. Shape into balls the size of a golf ball. Fry, a few at a time, in hot, deep oil until they are golden brown. Serve with a variety of sauces and dips.

Lion's Head
(for 4)

1½ lbs. pork (ham or shoulder)
5 dried Chinese mushrooms
⅓ cup bamboo shoots, chopped
1 large clove garlic, mashed
2 thin slices fresh ginger, minced
4 scallions, chopped
salt and pepper to taste
1 tsp. sugar
2 tbsp. sherry

1 tsp. cornstarch
1 egg, beaten
oil for deep frying
1 cup chicken broth
4 tbsp. soy sauce
1 small Chinese cabbage (about ¾ lb.)
1 tbsp. oil
2 tsp. cornstarch
1 tbsp. water

Chop the pork quite fine. Soak mushrooms in warm water for half an hour, remove and discard stems, squeeze dry and mince caps. Put chopped meat in a bowl. Add mushrooms, bamboo shoots, garlic, ginger root and scallions. Also salt, pepper, sugar, sherry, 1 teaspoon cornstarch and egg. Stir to blend mixture. Do not stir too much or the mixture will become too heavy. Shape into four balls. Heat oil in a deep pan and fry the pork balls for about 4 minutes or until lightly browned. Drain on paper towel and put them in a saucepan. Add broth and soy sauce, bring to a boil, reduce heat, cover and simmer for 25 minutes. Trim cabbage, cut into broad slices. Heat 1 tablespoon oil in a wok and stir-fry cabbage for a few minutes until soft. Then place cabbage on top of simmering pork balls, cover and simmer for 10 more minutes. Dilute cornstarch with water, add to sauce, stir until thickened. Put cabbage on serving dish, the pork balls on top, and cover with the sauce.

Deep Fried Pork Balls
(for 4)

1½ lbs. pork with some fat
    (boned loin, butt or
    shoulder)
⅓ cup bamboo shoots, minced
1 water chestnut, minced
1 slice fresh ginger root, minced
⅓ cup minced onion

1 clove garlic, minced
1 tsp. sugar
1 tbsp. soy sauce
1 tbsp. sherry
2½ tbsp. cornstarch
    egg
oil for deep frying

Mince the pork, mix with bamboo shoots, water chestnut, ginger, onion and garlic. Blend in sugar, soy sauce, sherry, cornstarch and the lightly beaten egg. Shape into about a dozen balls and chill for half an hour. Heat oil for deep frying. Fry, a few balls at a time, for about 3 minutes. Remove them and drain on paper towels. When all are fried, reheat the oil and fry the balls a second time, until they are browned and crisp. Drain again on towels and serve.

Braised Pork Chops
(for 4)

2 tbsp. oil
4 thick pork chops
1 small onion, thinly sliced
1 clove garlic, minced
⅓ cup soy sauce
2 tbsp. sherry

1½ cup chicken broth
½ tsp. sugar
1 lb. spinach, washed and
trimmed
2 tbsp. oil

Heat oil in a heavy casserole, brown pork chops quickly on both sides. Remove from pan and keep warm. Pour off most of the fat, stir-fry onions and garlic for 1 minute. Return pork chops, add soy sauce, sherry, broth and sugar. Bring to a boil, cover and simmer for half an hour. Turn chops over and simmer covered for another half hour. Heat 2 tablespoons oil in a wok, stir-fry spinach for a minute or two, just before pork is cooked. Put pork on a serving platter, surround with spinach and pour sauce over the meat.

Roast Pork I

(for 5-6)

1 cup water
4 tbsp. sugar
2 tbsp. light brown
   sugar
1 tbsp. salt
¼ tsp. pepper
¼ cup soy sauce

¼ cup sherry
1 tsp. vinegar
1 large clove garlic, minced
2 slices ginger root, minced
3 lbs. lean pork (shoulder, loin,
   butt, or fresh ham)

Heat water, stir in sugar until melted, remove from heat, add salt, pepper, soy sauce, sherry, vinegar, garlic and ginger root. Blend well and coat meat on all sides with the marinade. Cover, refrigerate and marinate meat for at least 24 hours, turning it occasionally. Remove meat from marinade, put on a rack in a roasting pan. Cook in preheated 450⁰ oven for 10 minutes. Reduce heat to 275⁰ and roast for 40 minutes, then turn meat and roast for another 40 minutes.

Roast Pork II
(for 4)

2 lbs. pork tenderloin or
  boned loin
1 large clove garlic, crushed
1 tbsp. grated onion
1 very thin slice ginger
  root, minced
3 tbsp. soy sauce
1½ tbsp. sherry

1 tbsp. hoisin sauce
freshly ground pepper to taste
2 tsp. sugar
¼ tsp. ground anise
½ tsp. (scant) cinnamon
pinch of allspice
2 tbsp. oil
2 tbsp. honey

Put pork in a pan. Blend all ingredients except honey and oil, add to the pork, coat the meat with it and let marinate for at least 3 hours. Drain and reserve the marinade. Place a shallow pan with water in bottom of the oven. Preheat oven to 425⁰. Put meat on a rack in a shallow roasting pan. Cook at 425⁰ for 15 minutes. Blend 2 tablespoons of the marinade with the oil and brush the meat on both sides with it. Reduce heat to 350⁰ and continue roasting for 20 minutes. Then brush both sides of meat with honey and roast 20 minutes longer.

To serve, cut into ¼ inch thick slices.

Red Simmered Pork

(for 4)

2 tbsp. oil
2 lbs. boneless pork
(ham, butt, or shoulder)
2 slices fresh ginger root,
minced
1 clove garlic, minced

2 scallions
$\frac{1}{3}$ cup soy sauce
3 tbsp. sherry
1 cup chicken stock
$1\frac{1}{2}$ cups boiling water
$1\frac{1}{2}$ tbsp. brown sugar

Heat oil in a heavy casserole, add pork and brown on all sides. Add ginger root, garlic, scallions cut into 1 inch pieces, soy sauce, sherry, chicken stock and water. Cover casserole, reduce heat and simmer 45 minutes. Turn the meat several times. Add the brown sugar and continue simmering for 45 minutes to an hour, turning the meat two or three times. Serve sliced with some of the sauce spooned over it.

Braised Spareribs and Pineapple
(for 4)

2 lbs. spareribs
1 clove garlic, minced
1 tsp. fresh ginger, minced
¼ cup soy sauce
¼ cup pineapple juice
3 tbsp. honey
¼ cup vinegar
½ cup chicken broth

2 tbsp. oil
1 tbsp. flour
1 cup canned pineapple chunks, drained
pinch of cayenne pepper
1 tbsp. cornstarch
1 tbsp. sherry
2 tbsp. water

Cut ribs apart and chop into 2½ inch pieces. Put in a bowl, add garlic, ginger and soy sauce, mix well and let stand for an hour. Blend pineapple juice, honey, vinegar, cayenne and chicken broth. Heat oil in a heavy saucepan. Drain ribs and stir-fry until well browned. Stir in flour and the pineapple juice mixture, bring to a simmer, cover and cook gently for 45 minutes. Blend cornstarch, sherry and water. Add pineapple chunks to meat, stir gently until heated through, stir in cornstarch mixture to thicken.

Stir-fried Spareribs, Sweet and Sour
(for 4)

2 lb. pork spareribs
4 tbsp. oil

1 cup sweet and sour sauce
(p. 154)

Chop ribs into 1 inch pieces, heat oil and stir-fry the ribs for about 8 to 10 minutes, until well browned. Heat sauce in a pan, drain spareribs on a paper towel, add to the sauce, coat well and serve.

Sub Gum Vegetables
(for 4)

1 green pepper
1 carrot
1 medium onion
3 stalks celery (white part only) sliced ½ inch thick
5 medium firm, fresh mushrooms
4 water chestnuts
½ cup bamboo shoots
3 scallions
½ cup bean sprouts, washed and dried
1 thin slice ginger root, shredded
1 clove garlic, minced
4 tbsp. oil
½ tsp. salt
3 tbsp. water
2 tbsp. soy sauce
1 tbsp. sherry
1 tsp. sugar
¼ tsp. sesame oil
1 tbsp. cornstarch
2 tbsp. water

Remove seeds and membrane from pepper, cut into 2 inch diamond shapes. Slice carrot into ¼ inch rounds. Cut onion lengthwise in half and the halves in ½ inch strips. Cut bamboo shoots and water chestnuts in ¼ inch slices, scallions into 1 inch pieces. Slice mushrooms ¼ inch thick.

Heat 2 tablespoons oil and salt in wok, stir-fry pepper and onion for half a minute. Remove and keep warm. Add another tablespoon of oil and stir-fry mushrooms and celery for 1 minute. Add bean sprouts and stir-fry 1 minute more. Remove from pan and keep warm. Add another tablespoon of oil to wok, fry carrot, bamboo shoots, ginger root, scallions, garlic and water chestnuts for 2 minutes. Add water, soy sauce, sherry, sugar and sesame oil, bring to a boil, return all vegetables to wok, heat to boiling and cook covered for 2 minutes. Dilute cornstarch with water, stir in until thickened.

Sub Gum Vegetables.→

Pork Lo Mein—See page 145 for recipe.→

Stuffed Eggplant
(for 2)

1 medium eggplant
½ lb. smoked (or cooked) ham,
   ground
1 slice fresh ginger, minced
1 clove garlic, minced
1 scallion, minced

2 tbsp. soy sauce
1 tbsp. sherry
½ tsp. salt
pepper to taste
½ tsp. sugar

    Cut eggplant lengthwise in half. Scoop out the seeds. Blend all other ingredients. Mound them in one half of the eggplant, cover with the other half. Place on a heatproof dish, steam for about half an hour until done. To serve, cut crosswise in sections.

←*Egg Foo Young*—See page 129 for recipe.

Stir-fried String Beans
(for 4)

1 lb. string beans
2 thin slices fresh ginger
  shredded
½ clove garlic, minced
1 scallion, chopped

1½ tbsp. soy sauce
¼ cup chicken broth
2 tsp. sugar
2 tbsp. oil
½ tsp. salt

String beans, wash and break them in 2 or 3 pieces. Heat oil and salt in heavy saucepan. Add ginger, garlic and scallion, stir-fry for a few seconds, add beans and stir to coat them with oil. Add all other ingredients, stir, cover and simmer for about 15 minutes. Stir them once while cooking.

Stir-fried Bean Sprouts

(for 4)

1 lb. bean sprouts
2 tbsp. oil
1 thin slice fresh ginger
   root, minced
1 stalk celery, white part,
   shredded
½ green pepper, seeded, membrane removed, shredded

4 scallions, shredded
½ medium onion, shredded
1 clove garlic, minced
⅓ cup shredded boiled ham
2 tbsp. chicken broth
1 tsp. cornstarch
1 tbsp. sherry

Scald bean sprouts with boiling water, let stand for half a minute, drain and dry well. Heat oil in a wok, add ginger root, stir-fry 30 seconds. Add celery, green pepper, scallions, onion and garlic, stir-fry 2 minutes. Add bean sprouts and ham, fry 30 seconds longer. Dilute cornstarch in chicken broth and sherry, stir in to thicken.

Stir-fried Chinese Cabbage
(Bok Choy)
(for 4)

1 slice fresh ginger, shredded
1 small clove garlic, minced
2 dried Chinese mushrooms
1 lb. Chinese cabbage, shredded
½ cup chicken broth
1 tbsp. soy sauce

pepper to taste
½ tsp. sugar
1½ tsp. cornstarch
1 tbsp. water
2 tbsp. oil
½ tsp. salt

Soak mushrooms for 15 minutes in warm water, discard stems, and shred caps. Heat oil and salt in a wok, add ginger and garlic and stir-fry for a few seconds. Add cabbage and mushrooms, stir-fry for 1½ minutes. Add combined chicken broth, soy sauce, pepper and sugar, bring to a boil and cook while stirring for 2 minutes until cabbage is just soft. Cover and simmer for 5 minutes. Dilute cornstarch with water and stir in to thicken.

Stir-fried Cauliflower
(for 4)

2 cups of trimmed cauliflower florets

2 tbsp. oil

2 thin slices fresh ginger root

2 scallions, minced

2 water chestnuts, thinly sliced

2 bamboo shoots, thinly sliced

1 stalk celery, white part, thinly sliced

½ cup chicken broth

1 tsp. oyster sauce

1 tbsp. sherry

1 tbsp. soy sauce

⅛ tsp. pepper

4 large shrimp, cooked, cut in chunks

2 tsp. cornstarch

1 tbsp. water

Blanch cauliflower in boiling salted water for 2 minutes. Drain and cool immediately under cold running water. Heat oil in a wok, add ginger and stir-fry for half a minute. Add scallions, water chestnuts, bamboo shoots and celery and stir-fry another half minute. Add cauliflower, stir-fry for 10 seconds then add chicken broth, oyster sauce, sherry, soy sauce and pepper. Bring to a boil, reduce heat, add shrimp, cover and simmer for 2 minutes. Dilute cornstarch with water, add and stir to thicken.

Stir-fried Celery, Bean Sprouts and Peppers

(for 4)

3 stalks celery, shredded
½ lb. bean sprouts
2 green peppers
2 tbsp. oil
½ tsp. salt
1 thin slice fresh ginger, minced

½ clove garlic, minced
¼ cup chicken broth
1 tbsp. soy sauce
½ tsp. sugar
1 tsp. cornstarch
2 tbsp. water

Wash bean sprouts, drain, cover with boiling water for 15 seconds, and drain again. Core and seed peppers and cut into thin strips. Heat oil and salt in a wok, add ginger and garlic, stir-fry for a few seconds, add celery and peppers, and fry for 1 minute. Add bean sprouts and fry for 1 minute more. Add chicken broth, soy sauce and sugar, stir well to blend, bring to a boil, cover and simmer for 3 minutes. Dilute cornstarch with water, stir in to thicken.

Cauliflower and Water Chestnuts
(for 4)

1 medium cauliflower
5 dried Chinese mushrooms
4 water chestnuts, sliced
½ cup chicken broth

2 tbsp. soy sauce
1 tsp. sherry
2 tbsp. cornstarch
¼ cup mushroom water
3 tbsp. oil

Trim florets off cauliflower and discard the core and stems. Put florets in a bowl, pour boiling water over them, let stand 5 minutes and drain.

Soak mushrooms in hot water for 15 minutes, discard stems, slice caps and save ¼ cup of the water.

Heat 2 tablespoons oil in a wok, add mushrooms and stir-fry for a few seconds. Add water chestnuts, fry for half a minute. Combine all other ingredients, except cauliflower, add to wok, stir and simmer for 2 minutes. Add cauliflower, stir, cover and simmer a few minutes longer, until florets are cooked but still somewhat crisp.

Stir-fried Savory Mushrooms
(for 4)

1 lb. small, firm, fresh mushrooms, sliced
2 tsp. fresh ginger root,
minced
2 scallions, minced
½ clove garlic, minced
2 tbsp. oil

½ tsp. salt
1 tbsp. soy sauce
1 tbsp. sherry
1 tsp. cornstarch
1 tsp. vinegar
pinch of cayenne pepper

Heat oil in a wok, add ginger root, scallions and garlic, stir-fry for half a minute. Add mushrooms and stir-fry for about 2 minutes or until just soft. Combine all other ingredients, stir into mushrooms, stir-fry quickly for half a minute and serve.

Stir-fried Spinach and Cashews
(for 4)

1 lb. spinach, washed and dried	½ tsp. sugar
¼ cup cashew nuts	⅓ cup chicken broth
½ clove garlic, minced	1 tsp. cornstarch
¼ cup Canadian bacon, chopped	2 tbsp. water
2 tbsp. soy sauce	3 tbsp. oil
1 tsp. sherry	½ tsp. salt

Wash spinach, remove coarse stems. Pour boiling water over spinach, let stand for 2 minutes, drain well, and chop coarsely. Chop nuts into fairly big pieces. Heat 2 tablespoons oil and salt in a wok, add garlic, stir-fry for a few seconds, add nuts, fry a few seconds longer. Add bacon, stir-fry a few seconds, add soy sauce, sherry, sugar and broth, stir, cover and simmer for 1 minute. In another pan heat remaining tablespoon of oil, add spinach and stir-fry until soft, about 2 minutes. Combine cornstarch and water, stir into spinach to thicken. Remove to serving platter and pour the contents of the other pan over the spinach.

Vegetable Medley
(for 4)

½ cup broccoli florets
¼ lb. string beans
½ cup celery, diced
½ cup bamboo shoots, diced
¼ lb. fresh mushrooms, sliced
1 slice fresh ginger, minced

1 clove garlic, minced
3 tbsp. oil
½ tsp. salt
½ cup chicken broth
1 tbsp. soy sauce
½ tsp. sugar

Blanch broccoli florets in boiling water for 10 seconds, drain. String beans and cut in 1 inch pieces, blanch in boiling water for 10 seconds, drain. Heat oil and salt in a wok, add ginger and garlic, and stir-fry for a few seconds. Add broccoli, beans and celery, fry for 2 minutes. Add bamboo shoots and mushrooms, stir-fry another 2 minutes. Combine broth, soy sauce and sugar, add to wok, stir well and bring to a boil. Cover and simmer for 2 minutes.

Bamboo Shoots and Mushrooms
(for 6)

5 tbsp. oil
2 cups bamboo shoots, sliced
   lengthwise
10 dried Chinese mushrooms
3 tbsp. soy sauce

1 tbsp. sherry
1 tsp. sugar
1 tbsp. cornstarch
¼ cup mushroom water

Soak mushrooms in 1 cup hot water for 15 minutes. Discard stems, slice caps, reserve the water they soaked in. Heat 3 tablespoons oil in a wok, stir-fry bamboo shoots for 2 minutes. Remove shoots and keep warm. Add remaining oil, stir-fry mushrooms for one minute, add soy sauce, sherry, sugar, and stir. Add bamboo shoots, cover and simmer for 2 minutes. Blend cornstarch with mushroom water, add to pan, stir to thicken.

Sweet and Sour Vegetables
(for 4)

1 small green pepper
3 stalks celery, sliced
1 medium onion
2 carrots
2 water chestnuts, sliced
3 tbsp. chicken broth
3 tbsp. vinegar
2 tbsp. sherry

2 tbsp. sugar
2 thin slices fresh ginger,
  minced
1 large clove garlic, crushed
½ cup shredded bamboo shoots
¼ tsp. pepper
1 tbsp. cornstarch
2 tbsp. water

Cut pepper in half, remove membrane and seeds. Cut into 2 inch long diamond shapes. Cut onion lengthwise in half, and then into ½ inch wide strips. Cut carrots diagonally into 1½ inch pieces. Heat oil in a wok, add ginger, garlic and carrots, stir-fry for a minute. Add pepper, onion, celery, water chestnuts and bamboo shoots, stir-fry over high heat for 2 minutes. Combine vinegar, sherry, broth, sugar and pepper and add to wok. Stir-fry 2 minutes more, cover and simmer for 2 minutes. Dilute cornstarch in water, stir in to thicken.

Spring Rolls
(Egg Rolls)
(about 16 skins)

2 eggs
2 cups water

2 cups flour
½ tsp. salt

Combine flour with lightly beaten eggs and salt. Add water gradually and beat until the batter is smooth. Grease a 7-inch skillet lightly with oil. Heat and pour a very small amount of batter into the pan, tilt the pan and swish the batter around to form a very thin layer. Pour off excess batter. Leave skillet on heat just long enough for the batter to set, barely one minute; do not let it brown. Remove from pan, put it on a plate and cover lightly with a damp cloth so that it won't dry out. Oil skillet lightly again and proceed to make the next skin.

Note: The skins can be made in advance. Many Chinese groceries carry commercially made skins.

How to cook Spring Rolls
(Egg Rolls)

1. *The filling,* whether stir-fried or other must be very dry. Squeeze it if necessary. A moist filling will cause the skins to break during cooking. Chill stir-fried fillings for half an hour before using.

2. *To fill* the skins, place about 3 tablespoons of filling slightly below the middle of the round skin. Fold the skin over, just to cover the filling, then roll tightly from the bottom up and tuck in the sides as you roll.

3. *To seal* the finished rolls, moisten the edges with a mixture of one tablespoon cornstarch and ½ cup cold water.

4. *To cook* the rolls, heat enough oil for frying to 375 degrees. Deep fry not more than 3 at a time, until they are golden brown and crisp. Drain on paper towels before serving.

   Spring rolls can also be pan fried in a wok or skillet. Heat 2 or 3 tablespoons of oil, add a couple of rolls and pan fry, turning them from time to time, until browned on all sides.

Stir-fried Ham and Shrimp Filling for Spring Rolls

½ lb. shrimp, shelled and deveined, cut in pieces
¼ lb. cooked or smoked ham,
shredded
½ cup celery, white part,
shredded
1 cup bean sprouts, washed
and parboiled for 3
minutes

2 scallions, chopped
3 water chestnuts, finely
chopped
1 clove garlic, minced
3 tbsp. oil
1 tsp. salt
½ tsp. sugar
1 tbsp. soy sauce

Drain parboiled bean sprouts well and dry with paper towel. Heat 1 tablespoon oil in a wok, add garlic, stir-fry a few seconds, add shrimp and ham, fry for 2 minutes, remove from pan. Add remaining oil, salt, sugar, soy sauce and the vegetables, stir-fry for 3 minutes. Return shrimp and ham to pan, fry one minute longer. Remove everything from pan, place in a sieve or colander and let drain for a few minutes, pressing down gently. Chill before wrapping.

Spring Roll Chicken Filling

1 chicken breast, boned
   and skinned
1 tsp. cornstarch
½ tsp. salt
½ tsp. sugar
1 tbsp. soy sauce

1 tbsp. sherry
3 tbsp. oil
3 scallions, chopped
1½ cups bean sprouts,
      parboiled for 3 minutes
¼ cup bamboo shoots, chopped

Cut the chicken in very narrow (julienne) strips. Put in a bowl, add cornstarch, salt, sugar, soy sauce and sherry. Mix well and let stand for 15 minutes. Heat 1 tablespoon oil in a wok, add chicken and stir-fry for 2 minutes. Remove chicken from pan. Add remaining oil, heat, add well-drained bean sprouts, scallions and bamboo shoots, stir-fry for 2 minutes. Return chicken to pan and fry 1 minute longer. Remove mixture from pan, put in a colander or sieve to drain, pressing down gently. Chill before using.

Egg Foo Young
(for 4)

5 eggs
1¼ tsp. salt
¼ tsp. pepper
½ cup onion, minced
1 small clove garlic, minced
½ cup bean sprouts, washed
and dried

3 scallions, chopped
½ cup celery, finely chopped
1 cup cooked pork or chicken,
diced
2 tbsp. soy sauce
4 tbsp. oil

Lightly beat eggs with salt and pepper; mix meat with vegetables and soy sauce and blend well with eggs. Heat oil in a wok and using a ladle or ¼ cup measure, drop mixture, one portion at a time, into the oil. Fry each portion as you would a small omelet until browned on both sides. Remove each as it is cooked and keep warm.

Sauce for Egg Foo Young

¾ cup chicken broth
salt to taste
1 tbsp. sherry
1 tbsp. soy sauce
1 tbsp. oyster sauce

1 tiny pinch cayenne
pepper
½ tsp. sugar
2 tbsp. cornstarch
1½ tbsp. water

Blend all ingredients except cornstarch and water. Simmer for a few minutes. Dilute cornstarch with water, blend into the sauce and stir to thicken.

Clam Egg Foo Young
(for 4)

5 eggs
1 tsp. salt
pinch of cayenne pepper
½ cup onions, minced
½ cup bamboo shoots, slivered
½ cup fresh mushrooms,
  sliced thin

½ clove garlic, minced
1 cup well drained canned
  minced clams or canned
  whole baby clams
2 tbsp. soy sauce
4 tbsp. oil

Beat eggs lightly with salt and cayenne pepper, blend well with all ingredients. Heat oil in a wok and using a ladle or ¼ cup measure, drop mixture into the oil, one portion at a time. Fry each portion as you would a small omelette, until brown on one side and nearly set. Fold over and cook a few seconds longer.

Ham and Egg Foo Young
(for 4)

½ cup bean sprouts,
blanched and dried

½ cup celery, white part
only, diced

¼ cup green peppers,
diced

¼ cup bamboo shoots, diced

½ tsp. onion, minced

2 scallions, chopped

¼ tsp. fresh ginger, minced
(opt.)

1 tsp. sherry

1½ tbsp. flour

1 tsp. salt

pepper to taste

1½ tbsp. oil

²/₃ cup cooked or
smoked ham, minced

6 eggs, beaten

4 to 5 tbsp. oil

1 tbsp. soy sauce

Heat 1½ tablespoons oil in a wok, add celery and bamboo shoots, stir-fry for a minute. Add bean sprouts, fry 1 minute. Add other vegetables, stir-fry 2 minutes. Stir in soy sauce, sherry, salt and pepper and stir-fry 1 minute more. Remove vegetables and let them cool. When cool, sprinkle with flour. Blend vegetables into beaten eggs, then blend in the ham. Add more oil to pan and heat well. Then cook mixture as in plain Egg Foo Young *(p. 129)*.

Shrimp Foo Young
(for 4)

4 eggs
salt and pepper to taste
1 tbsp. sherry
3½ tbsp. oil
1 water chestnut, minced
2 scallions, shredded
2 tsp. soy sauce

1 tbsp. celery, white part,
  shredded
²/₃ cup bean sprouts,
  blanched and dried
1 cup small shrimp, peeled
½ cup Foo Young sauce

Beat eggs lightly, mix in sherry, salt and pepper. Heat 1½ tablespoons oil in a wok, add scallions, water chestnut and celery, stir-fry for 1½ minutes. Add shrimp, bean sprouts and soy sauce and fry for 1 minute longer. Remove wok from heat, let mixture cool and stir in the eggs. Heat 2 tablespoons oil in a frying or omelet pan, add egg mixture and cook until lightly browned on the underside and nearly set. Fold the omelet and cook just a few seconds longer. Put omelet on a serving plate and serve with the Foo Young sauce.

Vegetarian Egg Foo Young
(for 4)

½ cup asparagus, cut
   pieces (use fresh or
   frozen)
½ cup string beans, par-
   boiled and sliced
1 cup celery, parboiled
   and sliced
½ cup onions, chopped
½ cup tomato, peeled, seeded,
   diced

½ clove garlic, minced
2 tbsp. soy sauce
1 tsp. salt
½ tsp. sugar
pepper to taste
1½ tbsp. oil
1½ tbsp. flour
5 eggs
4 tbsp. oil
¼ cup green pepper, diced

Add 1½ tablespoons oil to wok, heat, add celery and string beans, stir-fry half a minute. Add onions and garlic, fry one minute. Add pepper and asparagus, stir-fry one minute longer. Add tomato, soy sauce, salt, pepper and sugar, stir-fry one half minute longer. Remove vegetables from pan, cool. When cool sprinkle with flour and blend with beaten eggs.

Heat remaining oil in wok and proceed to cook as in plain Egg Foo Young *(p. 129).*

Eggs and Mushrooms
(for 4)

2 stalks scallions, chopped
½ small clove garlic, minced
2 tbsp. oil
5 eggs, beaten
½ cup slivered fresh
   mushrooms

pinch of cayenne pepper
salt to taste
½ tsp. vinegar
¼ tsp. sugar
1 tbsp. soy sauce

Beat eggs, blend in cayenne pepper, salt, vinegar, sugar and mushrooms. Heat oil in a wok, add scallions and garlic and stir-fry for a few seconds. Add eggs and fry, pushing them from the edges to center, until they are just set. Do not overcook. Sprinkle with soy sauce and serve.

Steamed Eggs and Ham
(for 4)

1 cup chicken broth
½ cup minced lean cooked or
  smoked ham
2 scallions, minced
½ small clove garlic, minced
1 tbsp. sherry

¼ tsp. sugar
salt and pepper to taste
1 tsp. oil
5 eggs
1 tbsp. soy or oyster sauce

Heat broth until hot, but not boiling. Blend ham, scallions, garlic, sherry, sugar, salt and pepper and oil. Beat eggs very lightly and blend gently with the meat mixture. Oil a shallow heatproof baking dish, pour in the egg mixture, and steam over boiling water for about 20 minutes until eggs have a custard-like consistency. After 15 minutes check with a toothpick or the point of a knife. If it comes out clean, the eggs are done. Sprinkle with soy or oyster sauce before serving.

Steamed Eggs and Oysters
(for 4)

5 eggs, very lightly beaten
1 tbsp. grated onion
1½ tsp. oil
2 tsp. sherry
½ cup oysters, drained
   and chopped

white pepper and salt
   to taste
¾ cup chicken broth
1 tbsp. oyster sauce
1 tbsp. finely minced scallions

Combine the very lightly beaten eggs with onion, oil, sherry, pepper and salt and the chopped oysters. Heat chicken broth but do not let boil. Combine the beaten egg mixture with the broth, a little at a time. Pour the mixture into a rather shallow, lightly oiled baking dish and steam over water for about 15 to 20 minutes, or until the eggs are set and custard-like. Sprinkle with oyster sauce and scallions before serving.

Note: Other seafoods or shellfish can be substituted for oysters.

Soy Colored Eggs

(for 4)

5 eggs
½ cup soy sauce
½ cup chicken broth

6 tbsp. sugar
1 tbsp. grated onion
1 tbsp. sherry

Put eggs in a saucepan, cover with water and boil gently for 10 minutes. Remove from water and cool under cold running water for 5 minutes. Shell carefully. Place eggs in a small saucepan, add all other ingredients, bring to a boil. Cover pan and simmer for 1 hour, turning the eggs several times during cooking so that they will color evenly. After one hour remove pan from heat, and cool eggs in their liquid for 30 minutes. Drain, quarter eggs lengthwise, serve on a bed of lettuce leaves with radishes.

Note: These eggs can be served as an attractive appetizer, or with meat or other dishes.

Tea Eggs
(for 4)

4 eggs
3 cups boiling water
2 tbsp. black tea

1 tbsp. salt
½ tsp. vinegar
1 clove star anise (opt.)

Put eggs in a pan with cold water, bring to a boil and simmer for 10 minutes. Remove eggs from pan, cool under cold running water for 5 minutes. Then tap the ends of the eggs gently, and roll them on a flat surface to crack the shells evenly. Do not remove the shells. Put 3 cups of boiling water in a small saucepan, add tea, salt, vinegar and anise, put eggs in the pan (the liquid should cover the eggs), and simmer for 1½ hours. Remove from heat and let stand for 1 or 2 hours. Then remove, shell and serve quartered or halved.

Note: Serve as appetizer or garnish.

To Cook Noodles

1 lb. egg noodles   1 tbsp. salt
2 quarts water   1 tbsp. oil

    Bring water to a boil, add salt and oil, add noodles, not too many at a time so that water keeps boiling. Boil uncovered for about 6 minutes or until noodles are cooked but still firm. Stir occasionally while cooking. When done, drain noodles and rinse quickly under running cold water. If they are to be used right away, drop them back into boiling water for just a minute until heated through, drain and serve. One can cook noodles in advance. When cooked, spread them in a large platter, sprinkle with a little oil so that they won't stick together. Reheat by dropping in boiling water and draining when hot.

Noodles and Meat Sauce
(for 4)

1 clove garlic, minced
1 slice fresh ginger, minced
4 scallions, minced
3 firm, fresh mushrooms, diced
¼ cup celery, minced
½ lb. lean pork, minced

2 tbsp. oil
½ tsp. salt
1 tbsp. soy sauce
1 tbsp. sherry
⅓ cup beef broth
1 tbsp. oyster sauce
1 lb. cooked egg noodles

Heat oil and salt in a wok, add garlic and ginger and stir-fry for half a minute. Add scallions and fry half a minute more. Add pork, stir-fry 2 minutes, then add mushrooms and celery and fry half a minute. Combine soy sauce, sherry, broth and oyster sauce. Add to wok, stir, cover and simmer for 3 to 4 minutes. Put hot noodles in a serving bowl, pour sauce over it.

Stewed Noodles
(for 4)

1 lb. egg noodles
¼ lb. smoked ham or Canadian bacon
1 small chicken breast, skinned and boned
½ lb. fresh shrimp, shelled and deveined
2 scallions, cut in ¼ inch lengths
1 clove garlic, minced
1 stalk celery, white part, shredded
1 tsp. fresh ginger, minced
2 tbsp. oil
1 tsp. salt
2 tbsp. soy sauce
1 tbsp. sherry
½ tsp. vinegar
1 tsp. cornstarch
2 cups chicken broth

Cook noodles for about 4 minutes. They should not be quite cooked through.

Cut ham and chicken into 1½ inch long strips. Cut shrimp into large pieces.

Heat oil and salt in a heavy pan or wok. Add scallions, celery, garlic, and ginger, stir-fry for a few seconds, add ham and chicken and stir-fry for 2 minutes. Add shrimp and fry an additional 2 minutes. Dissolve cornstarch in broth. Add broth, noodles and all other ingredients to pan, stir lightly to mix, cover and simmer for about 10 minutes.

Noodles and Pork Sauce
(for 4)

3 tbsp. oil
1 thin slice fresh ginger
   root, minced
1 clove garlic, minced
3 scallions, shredded
$\frac{1}{3}$ cup bamboo shoots, diced
$\frac{1}{3}$ cup fresh diced mushrooms

$\frac{1}{2}$ lb. lean pork, minced
$\frac{1}{2}$ tsp. sugar
1 tbsp. sherry
$1\frac{1}{2}$ tbsp. Bovril
$\frac{1}{4}$ cup beef broth
1 tbsp. hoisin or soy sauce
1 lb. egg noodles

Boil noodles in ample salted water; when done, rinse quickly under cold water, drain well, mix in one tablespoon of oil and keep hot.

Heat 2 tablespoons oil in a wok. Add garlic and ginger, stir-fry half a minute. Add scallions, fry half a minute, add pork and stir-fry $1\frac{1}{2}$ minutes until meat has lost any trace of pink. Add bamboo shoots and mushrooms, fry 30 seconds longer. Stir in sugar, sherry, Bovril, beef broth, and hoisin sauce. Reduce heat, cover and cook slowly for 5 minutes.

Serve noodles in individual bowls, spoon sauce over noodles.

Chicken Lo Mein
(for 4)

1 large chicken breast,
  boned and skinned
3 tbsp. oil
1 tsp. salt
1 cup Chinese cabbage,
  shredded
1 cup celery, sliced thin
1 cup bean sprouts, washed
  and blanched

2 tbsp. soy sauce
1 tbsp. sherry
½ tsp. sugar
1 cup chicken broth
1 tbsp. cornstarch
3 cups fine egg noodles,
  cooked and drained
3 scallions, minced

Cut chicken breast into thin strips. Pour boiling water over bean sprouts and drain.

Heat oil and salt in a saucepan, add chicken and stir-fry for 2 minutes. Add vegetables, soy sauce, sherry and sugar, stir well, cover and simmer for 3 minutes. Blend cornstarch into broth, add to pan and stir to thicken. Add cooked noodles, stir lightly and heat through. Put on serving platter and sprinkle with scallions.

Shrimp Lo Mein
(for 4)

¾ lb. raw shrimp
½ tsp. fresh ginger, minced
1 tbsp. cornstarch
1 tbsp. sherry
1 tbsp. soy sauce
1 tbsp. oyster sauce
pinch of cayenne pepper

⅔ cup Chinese cabbage,
    sliced thin
⅔ cup celery, sliced thin
4 fresh mushrooms, sliced
4 tbsp. oil
½ tsp. salt
1 lb. egg noodles, cooked

    Shell, devein and chop shrimp coarsely. Combine cornstarch, sherry, soy sauce, oyster sauce, cayenne pepper and ginger. Coat chopped shrimp with this mixture. Heat 2 tablespoons oil and salt in a wok, stir-fry shrimp for about 2 minutes, remove and keep warm. Add remaining oil, cabbage and celery, stir-fry for 2 minutes. Add mushrooms, stir, cover pan and cook gently for 2 minutes. Return shrimp to pan, stir until heated through. Pour shrimp and vegetable mixture over hot noodles and serve.

Pork Lo Mein
(for 4)

½ lb. egg noodles
¼ cup bamboo shoots
1 cup Chinese cabbage
6 firm, fresh mushroom caps
½ cup bean sprouts, blanched
1 small clove garlic, minced
¾ lb. Chinese roast pork

¼ cup chicken broth
1 tbsp. oyster sauce
1 tbsp. sherry
1 tsp. soy sauce
salt and pepper to taste
1 tbsp. oil

Boil noodles in ample water for about 5 minutes. Drain, rinse with cold water and reserve. Shred mushroom caps. Cut pork into fine shreds about 1½ inches long. Cut cabbage into 2 inch long slices. Cut bamboo into ¼ inch thick slices. Blanch with boiling water, drain and dry bean sprouts.

Heat oil in a wok, add bamboo shoots, cabbage, mushrooms, bean sprouts, garlic and pork. Stir fry for 3 minutes. Add chicken broth, blend, put noodles on top, cover and cook for 3 minutes. Mix oyster sauce, sherry, soy sauce; season with salt and pepper and add to wok. Stir, heat through and serve.

Basic Rice Cooking
(for 4)

Use Carolina or Patna (Texas) long grain rice. Pre-cooked and "instant" rice is not suitable for Chinese cooking.

1 cup rice
water

Place rice in a sieve and wash under running cold water, rubbing the grains with your fingers until the water runs clear. This removes excess starch and dust from the rice. Place rice in a pan, add enough water to cover rice by about 1 inch. Bring to a boil. Then cover the pan and simmer for about 25 minutes until rice is cooked and all liquid has been absorbed. While cooking, stir only once, gently, with a fork, but do not uncover the pan more than once.

Basic Fried Rice
(for 4)

4 cups cooked rice, cold
3 eggs, lightly beaten with
 1 tbsp. water
salt to taste
2 tbsp. oil

3 scallions, cut in ½ inch
 pieces
2 tbsp. soy sauce
1 tbsp. sherry

Stir rice with a fork to separate grains and break up lumps. Heat oil in wok, add salt and stir-fry scallions for 30 seconds. Add the rice and stir-fry until hot and each grain is coated with oil. Add eggs and stir-fry quickly until well blended and the eggs are nearly set. Blend in soy sauce and sherry. Serve piping hot.

Simple Fried Rice
(for 4)

4 cups cooked rice, cold
1 cup cooked meats (roast pork, chicken, etc. or cooked shellfish)
1 cup fresh, sliced or diced vegetables
4 scallions, cut in small pieces

2 eggs, lightly beaten
4 tbsp. oil
2 tbsp. soy sauce
1 tsp. sherry
½ tsp. sugar
salt to taste

Heat 2 tablespoons oil in a wok, add scallions, stir-fry a few seconds, add vegetables and stir-fry a minute or two until they are somewhat softened. Add meat or shellfish, blend well and stir-fry until hot. Remove vegetables and meat from wok and keep warm. Add remaining oil to wok, heat until quite hot, add rice (be sure that the grains are separate and that there are no lumps), stir-fry quickly until all grains are covered with oil. Return meat and vegetables to wok, blend well with a spoon or spatula. Mix in soy sauce, sherry, sugar and salt. Fold in eggs until they just begin to set. Serve immediately.

Eight Precious Fried Rice
(for 6)

4 cups cooked rice, cold
3 eggs, beaten with 1 tbsp. water
3 tbsp. oil
3 scallions, chopped
8 medium raw shrimp, shelled and deveined and chopped
½ cup raw diced chicken breast
½ cup diced lean pork

½ cup smoked ham, diced
4 fresh mushrooms, chopped
2 water chestnuts, thinly sliced
2 bamboo shoots, diced
½ cup cooked peas
1 tbsp. soy sauce
1 tbsp. sherry
1 tsp. salt

Heat oil in wok, add scallions, stir-fry half a minute. Add pork, stir-fry 2 minutes until all traces of pink have disappeared. Add chicken, ham and mushrooms, fry for 1 minute. Add shrimp, water chestnuts and bamboo shoots, stir-fry for another minute. Add rice, blend well and fry 1 minute. Add peas, soy sauce, sherry and salt, blend and fry until hot. Add eggs, blend quickly and stir-fry until they are just starting to set.

Shrimp and Lobster Tail Fried Rice

(for 4)

½ lb. shrimp, shelled and deveined

2 lobster tails (about ½ lb.)

2 eggs, beaten

1 cup fresh mushrooms, sliced

⅓ cup onion, chopped

1 tsp. fresh ginger, minced

3 cups cooked cold rice

4 tbsp. oil

2 tbsp. soy sauce

pinch of cayenne pepper

1 tsp. salt

Cut shrimp in half and shelled lobster tails in 1½ inch thick chunks. Heat 2 tablespoons oil in a wok or heavy saucepan, add ginger, stir-fry for a few seconds. Add shrimp and lobster meat and fry for about 2 minutes until it gets somewhat firm and pinkish in color. Remove from pan and reserve.

Add remaining oil to pan, heat and stir-fry mushrooms and onions for 2 minutes. Break up rice so that there are no chunks and the grains are separated. Add to pan, along with soy sauce, salt and cayenne pepper, mix well, stir until well heated. Return shrimp and lobster to pan and stir until hot. Fold in beaten eggs and stir until they are about set.

Vegetarian Fried Rice
(for 4)

1 clove garlic, minced
½ cup fresh mushrooms, sliced
½ cup bean sprouts, washed
  and blanched
½ cup onions, chopped
½ cup green peppers, diced
  small
¼ cup pimento (canned),
  chopped

2 scallions, chopped
2 eggs, beaten
4 cups cooked, cold rice
4 tbsp. oil
2 tbsp. soy sauce
1 tsp. salt
pepper to taste

Heat 2 tablespoons oil in a wok, add garlic and stir-fry for a few seconds; add onions and bean sprouts, fry for 2 minutes; add peppers and scallions, fry for 1 minute; add mushrooms and pimento and stir-fry 2 more minutes. Remove vegetables and keep warm. Add remaining oil to pan and heat. Break up rice so that there are no chunks and the grains are separated, add to pan along with soy sauce, pepper and salt. Stir-fry until well heated. Return vegetables, stir well and heat through. Fold in beaten eggs and stir until they are about set.

Hot Chinese Mustard

¼ cup powdered mustard
1 cup water
1 tbsp. sherry

2 tsp. vinegar
½ tsp. salt

Blend well, store in a tightly covered jar in refrigerator.

Dip for Cooked Shrimp

2 thin slices fresh ginger
  root, shredded
1 scallion, white part only,
  minced

4 tbsp. soy sauce
1 tbsp. sherry
2 tsp. vinegar
¼ tsp. mustard powder

Blend well.

Soy Dip Sauce for Chicken

2 tbsp. oil
1 tsp. finely minced scallions, white part only
⅛ tsp. mashed garlic
1 tbsp. sherry

½ tsp. finely minced
  ginger root
4 tbsp. soy sauce
¼ tsp. vinegar

Blend well, cover and simmer for 1 minute. Cool before serving.

Marinade for Barbecued Pork

½ cup broth (chicken or beef)
2 tsp. Bovril
1 tbsp. honey
1 tbsp. brown sugar
1 tbsp. soy sauce

1 clove garlic, finely
 minced
2 tbsp. sherry
¼ tsp. allspice
salt to taste

Combine in a saucepan stock, Bovril, honey, sugar, and garlic. Heat gently and stir until blended. Add all other ingredients.

Marinade for Barbecued Spareribs

2 slices fresh ginger root,
 minced
2 cloves garlic, minced
¼ cup soy sauce

¾ cup broth (chicken or beef)
2 tbsp. honey
2 tbsp. sherry
1½ tbsp. vinegar

Blend all ingredients, coat spareribs and marinate 2 hours.

Sweet and Sour Sauce

¾ cup chicken stock
¼ cup honey
¼ cup brown sugar
½ cup vinegar
1 tbsp. cornstarch
1 tbsp. soy sauce
1 tsp. Bovril

2 tbsp. sherry
3 tbsp. water
1 large clove garlic, finely
   minced
1 tbsp. lemon juice
pinch of cayenne pepper

Bring chicken stock to a boil, add honey and sugar, stir until dissolved, then add the vinegar, garlic, lemon juice, Bovril and cayenne pepper. Blend cornstarch with soy sauce, sherry and water, add to liquid and stir until thickened.

Oyster Sauce

If bottled oyster sauce cannot be found, here is a fairly simple way to approximate the imported product:

12 oysters (or 8 ounces frozen)
½ cup oyster liquor
1½ tbsp. soy sauce

Open oysters, reserve liquor. Mince oysters, strain the liquid through a fine sieve. Put oysters and liquor in a small saucepan, bring to a boil, and simmer, covered for about 20 minutes. Strain through a fine sieve, discard oyster meat. Stir soy sauce into the strained liquor. Keep refrigerated.

Eight Precious Pudding
(for 6-8)

1½ cups rice
1 cup mixed candied fruit
⅔ cup pitted dates
⅔ cup blanched almonds
⅔ cup raisins

1 cup red bean paste*
½ cup sugar
2 tbsp. oil
simple sugar syrup (opt.)

Put rice in a strainer and wash under running water until water runs clear. Put rice in a pan, add 4 cups of water, cover, bring to a boil. Boil for 5 minutes, then reduce heat and cook for 20 minutes, until water has been absorbed and rice is cooked. Blend in sugar and oil. Oil a heatproof bowl and arrange fruits, raisins and nuts in a neat pattern in the bottom of the bowl. Spoon half the rice into the bowl, being careful not to disturb the fruit pattern. Firm down gently with the back of a spoon. Spread the bean paste on top but don't spread the paste to the edge of the bowl; keep it 1 inch away from the sides. Add remainder of rice to the bowl, pack it down gently, cover bowl with aluminum foil and steam for about 45 minutes. Invert bowl on a serving platter and serve with hot syrup.

*Available in Chinese food markets.

Glazed Honey Apples
(for 4)

2 or 3 firm apples
¾ cup flour
1 egg, beaten
½ cup water
1 cup sugar

2 cups water
½ tbsp. lemon juice
1 tbsp. oil
oil for deep frying

Combine flour, water and egg to make a smooth batter.

Prepare a syrup: Put 1 tablespoon oil in a heavy pan, add sugar, water and lemon juice and heat until the syrup reaches the "crack" stage or 275° on a candy thermometer.

Core and pare apples, cut into thick wedges, dip in batter and deep fry, drain on paper towel. Coat well with the hot syrup.

Coat a serving platter with oil to prevent the apple pieces from sticking; put the apples on the platter. Serve with a bowl of ice water.

To eat: Pick up the hot apple slices with chopsticks or small skewers, dip them in the ice water, which will harden the syrup, but the apple inside will be soft and hot.

‡ Note: Banana pieces can be substituted for apple.

Peking Dust
(for 6)

1 lb. can of unsweetened
   chestnut puree
¼ cup sugar
1½ cups heavy cream
3 tbsp. sugar

1 tsp. vanilla extract
2 tbsp. brandy
glacéed fruit
blanched almonds

Blend chestnut puree with ¼ cup sugar. Whip cream with vanilla and the 3 tablespoons of sugar. Blend in brandy. Blend half of the whipped cream with the chestnut puree. Oil a small bowl lightly, put chestnut mixture in the bowl, press down to fill the bowl evenly. Then invert the bowl on a serving platter to remove the chestnut cream. Pipe remaining whipped cream over the chestnut mixture with a pastry tube, or smooth it over with a spatula. Decorate with glacéed fruit and almonds.

Index